Vinod Taylor,

with good

tacanting

..

1 may 2003

Education for a Global Society

Foreword

Despite the astounding scientific and technological developments during the 20th century, humanity remains fractured and fragmented, torn by turmoil and tension. The notion that technological change and economic growth by themselves can ensure a peaceful and sane global society is seriously challenged, and unfortunately many of the present conflicts on the planet can be traced back to age-old rivalries between the great religions around the world. One would have expected that we would learn from the gory history of inter-religious strife over the centuries and move towards a more inclusive and tolerant approach to the inter-religious dialogue, but this has not happened.

The Interfaith movement, which can be said to have begun in modern times with the first Parliament of the Worlds' Religions in Chicago in 1893 and which saw the development of several Interfaith organisations and Conferences around the world during the last century, has as its goal the furthering of harmony and understanding between the great religious traditions of humanity. One of the premier organisations is the Temple of Understanding which was founded in 1960 by a remarkable American woman, Juliet Holister. Since its inception the Temple of Understanding has been in the forefront of the Interfaith movement. While its headquarters are in New York, we have had an active India Chapter now for many years, and despite lack of financial resources we have pursued our activities in Delhi and in other Centres around the country.

Education being the key to Interfaith understanding, we decided to set up a Interfaith Consultation on Education for a Global Society in which we were expecting about 40 delegates from the United States and a similar number from India. The dates for the

Conference were fixed for early in January 2002, but in 2001 the September 11 disaster in the United States and the subsequent security problems led us to decide that we would have two separate Consultations—one in the United States and one in India, both of which were subsequently held.

The Indian Consultation was held on January 4-5, 2002 and the present volume is based upon the papers received on that occasion, and also significant verbal interventions made during the course of the Consultation. The Volume is edited by the Convenor, Prof Marmar Mukhopadhyay. It is my hope that this volume will be of practical utility to educationists around the world who are beginning to appreciate the importance of imparting Interfaith values to the younger generations if humanity is ever to break out of the negative factors that have dogged it for centuries and move towards a sane and harmonious global society.

31 January 2003   **Karan Singh**

ISBN 81-7541-148-1

First Published in India in 2003

Education for a Global Society: Inter-faith Dimensions

© The Temple of Understanding

Published by:
SHIPRA PUBLICATIONS
115-A, Shakarpur, Vikas Marg
Delhi-110092, INDIA
Phone: 22458662, 22500954
Fax: 91-11-22458662
E-mail: siprapub@satyam.net.in
www.shiprapublications.com

Laser Typesetting at:
Kumar DTP Systems
Delhi-110091

Printed at:
Choudhary Offset Process
Delhi-110051

Education for a Global Society
Inter-faith Dimensions

Foreword by
Dr. Karan Singh

Edited by
Marmar Mukhopadhyay

The Temple of Understanding

Preface

This volume contains selected presentations in the *International Consultation on Inter-faith Dimension in Education for Global Society* chaired by Dr. Karan Singh, hosted by The Temple of Understanding. I am grateful to Dr. Karan Singh for inviting me to convene the consultation, and entrusting the responsibility of editing the selected presentations.

The relevance of the Consultation became evident from the fact that about fifty American Educators who were to participate in this consultation had to stay back because of the September 11, 2001 event.

The world is being pulled by two competing forces. On one hand, the forces of globalisation are bringing countries closer to each other; on the other hand, more and more countries are declaring themselves as religious nation-states, pulling them away from each other. The globalisation is still almost one-dimensional, and that is economic. The information and communication technology that cut across national boundaries is bringing cultures closer and closer.

The interesting paradox of our times is that it is the religions that have professed the fundamental unity of the human beings; the nature of human has been defined as either God's own child or God's representative on earth by almost all the religious traditions. Yet, it is the religious fundamentalism devoid of the understanding of the basic spirits of the religious traditions that stands on the way of global unity. On the other hand, the cultures, the social mores and practices, the economic activities that have been conventionally the dividing lines and forces among people, not only between and among the nations but also among different groups of people within the nation, are creating the new global village through cultural and economic unity.

The power of religion, particularly the religious faith, must be understood very clearly today than ever before. Leaving alone a tiny group of few people who claim themselves atheists, many of whom offer prayers to Almighty in private, people all over the globe are basically religious, a very large majority of them living in secular states. For, there is no clash between people being religious in a secular state. Secular states do not preach absence of or religions or the religious faiths. Instead, they profess respect for all religious traditions and faiths. Such approach to secularism is strongly supported by the wisdom literature from all religious traditions in the world that professes that all roads sincerely traversed leads to God.

At a time, when instruments of mass destruction are extremely powerful, mutual respect for religious traditions and faiths, indeed interfaith is only hope for survival of human civilisation on this beautiful earth. If globalisation of the human civilisation is unstoppable, earlier we realise the role of interfaith, better it is for us. Symbolically, the global society can stand only on the interfaith as its foundation. The Nigerian Minister, during the E-9 Summit in Delhi in 1993, rightly said that education is not only the best defence but the only defence today. Education can be a powerful instrument of defence only by building in the interfaith dimension in it. Interfaith education offers an important key to the installation of peace in human mind. If war is in the minds of men (UN Charter), we must find means to sow seeds of peace in human minds. Education offers the best bet.

Marmar Mukhopadhyay

Contents

Inter-faith Values for Education for a Global Society

Karan Singh

As we moved through the last decade of the preceding century, which witnessed unparalleled destruction and unimagined progress; the cruellest mass killings in human history and the most outstanding breakthroughs in human welfare; the advent of weapons of unprecedented lethality and the creative probing into outer space, we find ourselves poised at a crucial crossroads in the long and tortuous history of the human race on Planet Earth. In our own lifetimes time have telescoped, both for better and for worse. While scientific applications has raised living standards for millions beyond all expectations, the problems of humanity have also assumed global dimensions and millions still go hungry day after day. The persistence of nuclear testing and the disposal of nuclear wastes, the dangers of global warming and the attenuation of our ozone shield, the menace of deforestation and the destruction of many species of flora and fauna, the extensive air and water pollution and the poisoning of the food chain, the malign underworld of drugs and the alarming spread of communicable diseases, are now problems which the human race shares in common, and which are simply not amenable to solution on anything less than a global footing.

It is now quite clear that humanity is transiting into a new kind of society, a transition even more significant than the earlier ones from the caves to the forests, from the forests to nomadic, pastoral, industrial and then to the post industrial society. What we are now witnessing, though we may be too close to the event to fully grasp its significance, is the transition to a global society. The future is upon us almost before we realise that the past has disappeared, and we find ourselves precariously poised in a present full of challenge and change. Whether it is political events or economic decisions, commercial or industrial activity, computer technology or space exploration, food and dress habits or the universal musical beat, all these have ceased to respect the artificial barriers imposed by national boundaries, and impelled by science and technology, have become global in their manifestation. We live in a shrinking world in which the malign heritage of conflict and cut throat competition, and the growing gap between the developed and the developing world, will have to make way for a new culture of convergence and co-operation if the rich promise of this new millennium is not to evaporate in conflict and chaos which is already overtaking many parts of the world.

It is not as if we lack the intellectual or economic resources to tackle the problems. Scientific breakthroughs and technological ingenuity have given us the capacity to overcome all these challenges. What is missing is the wisdom and compassion to do so. Knowledge proliferates, but wisdom languishes. It is this yawning chasm that will need to be bridged if we are ever to reverse the present trend towards disaster, and it is here that education in the broadest sense of the term assumes such a vital position. Unfortunately, all our national educational systems are postulated on beliefs that flow from pre-nuclear and pre-global perceptions, and as a result are quite unable to provide the new paradigm of thought that human welfare and survival now requires. Outmoded orthodoxy and obsolescent orientations continue to deprive the younger generations of an adequate awareness of the essential unity of the world into which they have been born. Indeed, by fostering negative attitudes towards other religious and cultural groups or nations, they hinder the growth of globalism.

We need to develop carefully structured programmes on a global scale based clearly and unequivocally on the premise that human survival involves the growth of a creative and compassionate global consciousness. The spiritual dimension will have to be once again given importance in our new educational thinking. Recently, I saw a quotation from President Jacques Delors where he said: "If in the next ten years we do not succeed in giving a soul, a spiritual selfhood, and a meaning to Europe, our efforts will have been in vain." If we substitute 'the world' for 'Europe', we get a clear statement of the challenge before us.

Creative educational thinkers have propounded holistic and human-oriented philosophies of education. In India alone we have had outstanding men like Sri Aurobindo, the great seer-philosopher and Rabindranath Tagore, the Nobel Laureate Poet; Mahatma Gandhi, the apostle of non-violence and J. Krishnamurti, the eminent thinker; Dr. Zakir Hussain, great educator-statesman, all of whom developed their theories of education and tried to put them into practice. These and other experiments in creative education elsewhere can be a source of inspiration and guidance to us in our task of structuring a new educational philosophy based on Inter-faith understanding for the new millennium. The Temple of Understanding has provided important leadership in this area.

Temple of Understanding and Inter-faith Movement

The Temple of Understanding was founded 40 years ago by an American woman, Juliet Hollister, who passed away only last year. It is an inter-faith organisation. The Inter-faith movement can be said to have begun in modern times in 1893 when the first Parliament of Worlds' Religions was held in Chicago. That was the one to which, by a concatenation of events, Swami Vivekananda arrived; he was not a delegate but it so happened that he reached there and spoke several times at the Congress and made a very big impact. There were 6000 delegates there in 1893, at the end of the 19th century.

During the 20th century, several inter-faith organisations grew—the International Association for Religious Freedom, the World Council of Religions, the Temple of Understanding, the United Religions Initiative and the Chicago group also became active again. There were a whole series of inter-faith meetings around the world in the last century, many of which, over the last 30 years, I had the privilege to attend in Moscow, in Oxford and at various places around the world.

In 1993, the Second Parliament of the Worlds' Religions was held in Chicago again, exactly a hundred years after the first one. I, along with many other friends from India attended the meeting. In 1999, the Third Parliament of the Worlds' Religions was held in Cape Town (South Africa). A remarkable event occurred in 2000; the United Nations called a meeting—The Millennium World Peace Summit for Spiritual and Religious Leaders. It was held in the main hall of the United Nations building, and I had the privilege of presiding over the First Plenary Session.

The point is that in the 20th century the Inter-faith movement began to grow, but it is still basically peripheral, it is not yet a central movement. My hope is that in the same way as the environmental movement moved from the periphery to the centre of human concern, the inter-faith movement too will become central in years to come. In 1982, at the first conference on the Human environment in Stockholm, only two Heads of Government—Indira Gandhi and Olof Palme, attended. In 1992, in Rio, 112 Heads of States participated, because environment had moved from the periphery to the centre of human consciousness. Our hope is that Inter-faith also will now move from the periphery to the center. A lot of work is being done in the various faiths. Beautiful temples are built, so are Mosques, Gurudwaras, Churches, and places of worship of other religious traditions. But the Inter-faith movement, as such, is yet nobody's baby. Unless the Inter-faith movement comes center stage, things are not going to fall into place. Education provides a sound platform for nurturing this inter-faith movement that is so very crucial for the global society.

Global Society

This global society is something which is now an evolutionary imperative. Science and technology has given us now the means to bring about a truly global society. However, the process of globalisation ' has got both benign and malign implications. Globalisation by itself is not an undiluted blessing. Of course, it has tremendous advantages in trade, in commerce, in the unity of human race. Sri Aurobindo's whole thesis of the Ideal of the

Human Unity, the ancient wisdom of *Vasudhaiva Kutumbakam*, can become a reality only because of the breakthroughs in technology, communications, satellites and so on.

On the other hand, terrorism has become global, trafficking on human being has become global, trafficking in drugs has become global, pandemics and sexually transmitted diseases have become global. There is a lot of negativity in globalism as there was in the pre-global society. So to assume that globalisation is necessarily good and benign is not good enough, and yet, globalisation is inevitable and universal.

So, the question is not 'whether or not we are going to have a global society', the question is, what sort of global society are we going to have? Are we going to have a global society based upon exploitation, based upon negativities, based upon crime, based upon hatred and based upon fanaticism, or are we going to have a sane and harmonious global society? That really is the question that faces us.

To try and turn the clock back and to hide from the emerging global society is futile. To build a wall around ourselves, cancelling television channels, putting up censorship are no longer feasible or even physically possible. We cannot build a wall preventing a satellite-eye. So, we have to bring a positive element into the global society.

Education for Global Society

For that purpose education is a critical input. And our consultation is specifically aimed at education for the global society. Education has to be at two levels—one is formal education, whether it is the conventional learning system or the open learning system. The second is public education—educating the public at large. If we wait until children who are now in primary school grow up, it will be too late. We have to educate the adults, the general public also. And that is where the open schools and open universities can offer a creative link between formal and public education.

In our definition education is a lifelong process. It does not stop with the end of a formal educational career. It begins at birth, some say even before birth, as the story of Abhimanyu tells us, and now scientists also say that even unborn babies respond to harmonious sounds. Thus education is a lifelong process all the way up to death. Our concern at this moment is education for the Inter-faith dialogue.

Inter-faith values are essential for a global society. What Inter-faith values are and how we can abstract them from the various religious traditions of the world, is something that requires very close attention. This is of special importance for India, where the official ideology is of a secular state. Secularism does not mean being anti-religion, but it also does not mean a single religion predominating over all the others. A fine balance needs to be struck. There is no doubt that Hinduism—chronologically, historically, philosophically, demographically in almost every way— is a predominant force in India, in the same way as Islam is in the Arab World or Roman Catholicism in Latin America. But there are some other streams. Jainism and Buddhism have made their own special input into our philosophical thinking. Sikhism was a deliberate attempt to try and bridge the gulf between Hinduism and Islam. These are the four Indic religions, the religions born in India. Then we have had five religions come to us from West Asia— Christianity, which arrived here a thousand years before it reached Europe and fifteen hundred years before it reached America with St Thomas in 57 a.d. Through schools and colleges, it has made a major impact on modern India. We have had Judaism, a small but significant population in Cochin, Kerala. Many of them left when Israel was set up. There are the Zarathustrians—small in numbers but with a very significant contribution to India. Then a thousand years interaction with Islam, some of it very negative, some of it very positive. Now, more recently there has been the *Baha'i* faith, which seems to be a sort of an Islamic Vedanta. It reminds us of Kahlil Gibran and of the Sufis and the mystics, with many of the *Vedantic* concepts.

There are twelve major religions recognised by the world community and each has got hundreds of sects; there are 128 churches, 72 sects in Islam and hundreds of sects in Hinduism. There is Shinto in Japan, Taoism in China and Confucianism in the

East. So Inter-faith values in India must try and include as broad a spectrum of values as possible. A small booklet titled *Unity in Diversity* with extracts from different religions of the world offers a meaningful glimpse in inter-faith values. So, the first element is education in inter-faith values.

The second is education for Environmental values, because in any global society, if the globe itself is destroyed, if the earth is destroyed, you cannot have a global society. Television reports of fires raging in Australia, the global warming in Europe and ice caps melting, ozone layer depleting, are horrifying. An important publication *Religion and Conservation* documents the Inter-faith declarations on Man and Nature by the major religions of the world. This contains what the religions of the world say on environment. This began in 1986 with five declarations one of which was written by me. Later in Assisi, the *Baha'is* Declaration, the Jain Declaration and others were added. There are nine declarations here. Yoga is also a conservation of the inner environment. So conservation and the environment can be looked upon both as the outer and the inner. We have to have our inner environment also conserved. If we are constantly poisoning ourselves with alcohol, drugs and such other things, our inner environment will be destroyed. Similarly the outer environment also needs to be cared for.

The third major area is education for socially desirable values. For example, punctuality. It does not belong to any particular religion. Hindus have the *Muhurtha*. Strictly speaking, the *Muhurtha* is so punctual, that if you miss it by one second, you have missed it. Punctuality is a socially desirable value. It is not a religious value. Or cleanliness, or respect for elders, or helpfulness, or compassion, or love, you can call them Inter-faith, but you do not have to be religious to adopt these values. In the West, they are meticulously punctual. They may not be religious, but they recognise the importance of time.

Socially desirable values are particularly important. In a country like ours, millions of people live in poverty; millions of children go to bed without one square meal a day; millions are drenched in the monsoons, shiver in the winter, and burn in the summer, without a proper place to stay. We are oases of affluence in a vast ocean of poverty, and those of us who have been born in fortunate circumstances should never forget our debt to society. So, these are what can be broadly included under the rubric of socially desirable values. Education for Inter-faith values, education for environmental values, education for socially desirable values taken together represent education for the global society.

Conclusion

In conclusion, we must pioneer a new holistic educational philosophy based upon certain chosen premises. The differences of race and religion, nationality and ideology, sex and sexual preference, economic and social status—though significant in themselves—must be viewed in the broader context of global unity. To preserve the ecology of Planet Earth, there should be a more equitable consumption pattern based on limits to growth, not unbridled consumerism. The world's great religions must no longer war against each other for supremacy, but mutually co-operate for the welfare of the aspiration that binds them together, that impels a continuing and creative inter-faith dialogue.

We must strive for a literate world with a concerted drive to eradicate the scourge of illiteracy world-wide, with special attention towards female literacy, particularly in the developing countries, so that the accumulated distortions of the past can be rectified, and the empowerment of women can be achieved which is so necessary for an integrated and harmonious civilisation.

Finally, the new holistic education based on inter-faith dialogue must include the multiple dimensions of the human personality—physical, intellectual, aesthetic, emotional and spiritual—and seek a harmonious development of an integrated human being with a value orientation.

Educatedness for the Global Society

Marmar Mukhopadhyay

The burden of this paper is to lay down the inter-faith basis of education for the global society of the new millennium; and propose a new paradigm of education—Educatedness for the global society. Viewing this through the prism of 'systems approach' offers us a meaningful vision where 'inter-faith base' is the input, 'education' is the process and output is a more humane civic global society. Relevant and pertinent as elsewhere, application of systems approach in this context implies education to be designed to create the global society of our choice, but informed by inter-faith considerations. To begin with the end, what is the nature of the global society in the new millennium?

The last century of the last millennium is crowned with heights of human ingenuity—both in 'gold' (bright) and 'lead' (dark). The breathtaking developments and breakthroughs in science and technology have simultaneously enriched and equipped human society and its system of governance with tools and techniques of information and communication technology, aviation and space technology, cloning and life saving drugs and host of such others that have significantly contributed to enrichment of quality of life. Simultaneously, it has offered lethal weapons of mass destruction. Events depicting human intentions are equally glaring on both sides—for example, spontaneous international response to epidemics, earthquakes and floods that represent human sufferings anywhere in the world is coupled with dark events in Hiroshima, Nagasaki, Chechnya, Bosnia, Afghanistan, Iraq. The last few decades of the last century witnessed a dangerous trend where more and more countries became equipped with lethal nuclear, biological and chemical weapons, not commensurate with their development status; further, such proliferation of destructive capabilities were not commensurate with developments that contribute to enrichment of quality of life. It is for the mere survival of the human society, it is necessary to conceptualise and work towards a global society. In the contemporary world that is torn with strife and wars, it may appear to be a utopia; nevertheless it is, as mentioned in the report of the International Commission on Education for 21st Century, a 'necessary utopia'. For, the human genii and prospect of its further growth in the new millennium will be fully competent to wipe out life on the mother earth by just pressing of a button. Education is the best defence, not only for cross border tension and terrorisms but also against the threat to human existence through 'learning to live together' with mutual trust, love, respect and concern.

That can be possible only when entire humanity irrespective of their geographical belongingness, languages spoken, and religions, mores, customs etc. practised is seen as a large human family. The Hindu religious tradition maintained several millennia ago—*Udaara Caritaanaantu Vasudhaiba Kutambakam* (for large hearted people, entire world is a family). This is equally pronounced in Sikhism:

> *Man apune te bura mitana*
> *Pekhai sagal srist(i) sajna (Astapadi 3, Saloka 6, Sacred Sukhmani)*

I guess, the rider—*udaara caritam* is the charter of education for the global society. It is from this angle that we should build the new educational paradigm.

Conventionally, educational paradigms are built around educational goals in terms of learning outcomes, courses and contents, methods of transaction of curricular contents, and evaluation. The emphasis is decidedly and probably exclusively on excellence in cognitive domain that equips one with intellectual competence, neutral to socio-emotional aspects of life of self and society. This is grossly inadequate for the global society that can be hospitable with steadily improved quality of life. It is here that we need to derive our inspiration from the inter-faith movement. Religious literature, except for religious education, rarely goes into nitty gritties of contents and processes of education, organisation and management of education. We will build our thesis around the concept of educatedness for the global society inspired by interfaith considerations.

The business of education has conventionally been defined as 'shaping of mind'; it is indeed, shaping of the 'human'. For, mind is just one of the components of a human being. That intricate process of shaping the human is the movement towards educatedness. Should educatedness be construed to be a forward movement of human nature, there is definite scope for reviewing the fundamentals of human nature—its potentials and propensities; for the nature and purpose of education is to progressively unfold the human potential and optimise it for individual and social goals.

Nature of Human Being

There are several discernible sources where nature of human being can be derived from. Religious literature is probably the single most important original source since these are revealed wisdom—*para vidya* in *Upanishidic* definition or knowledge through acquaintance by modern epistemology (Bertrand Russel). *Al-Quran* was revealed to Prophet Mohammad, Vedas were revealed to Saints and Seers. Gautam Buddha's self-realisation was the source of his prophetic wisdom on human nature. There are interesting points of convergence on the issue of nature of humane beings:

- Humans, in Hindu tradition, have been described as child of God (*Amritasya Putraha*).
- According to Islam, "Man is God's Viceroy on earth."
- "God is the soul of man, his eternal nature," says Sikhism.
- According to Christianity, "Man is God's workman on earth."
- "The Wise One created man to be like Him", contends Zoroastrianism.
- According to the *Baha'is*, "Man is the supreme Talisman".
- Jain contention is, "Man is creation of God, made in the likeness of God".
- "Heaven has made man good. His original nature is good..." is the contention of Confucianism.

It would be evident that, in all the religions, humans have been defined, in one way or other, as child or representative of God. Kahlil Gibran, in his famous poetic work. *The Prophet* told the parents that "The child is *through* you" and *from the God.* This indicates the essential unity of all religions—*Ekam Sad Vipraha Bahudha Vadanti (Rig Veda)* or Wherever you turn, there is the face of God *(Quran)* (Karan Singh, 2000).

The major implication of accepting the proposition that human is indeed the child of God, is that every human has the potentiality of achieving immortality, that is the attribute of God himself/herself. Leonard Orr, the Christian Spiritual Leader, in his interesting treatise *Breaking the Death Habits* argued that humans are basically immortal, that is the attribute of God. He, however, added that humans develop the habit of dying.

This Divinity in humans is however not apparent. Coats and coats of colours, habits, hide the propensities. In *Baha'i* view, "lack of proper education hath, however, deprived him of that which he doth inherently possess". Thus in the real world we experience humans positioned on a continuum between beastliness and divinity, the two ends of the continuum. In social terms, beastliness is indicated by the instinct of acquisitiveness—tendencies of acquisition of material wealth and comfort. Religious scriptures also describe hunger, sleep, procreation, fear, anger etc. as indicators of beastliness.

Divinity, on the other hand, is indicated by renunciation—giving away for the benefit and happiness of others. The saints and seers are characterised by their nature of giving away all that they have. Sadhu Vaswani's life is an instant example where he gives away his meagre belonging to others in need. Crucifixion of Jesus, martyrdom of Guru Tegh Bahadur, and innumerable instances of Hindu saints relieving sufferings of fellow beings by taking away their diseases on to themselves are some of the outstanding examples where life itself was given away for the benefit of others. In poetic expression,

> *"When you see a thorn on path lies,*
> *Take it up, and a flower let there be;*

A thousand thorns you will have thus uprooted,
The road with flowers strewn smiling stand."

(The Muse' by NP Mukherjee)

In reality, it is not difficult to pick up the thousand thorns and leave the road smiling with flowers. It is a matter of value. The beastly behaviour is indicated by picking up the flowers, leaving the road with thorns for others to walk on, whereas divinity is in picking up the thorns despite the risks of being hurt. Humans move, across births, from one end of the continuum to the other. Importantly, every human being has the potentiality to move from where he/she is towards the ultimate destination—the Divinity. Shri Aurobindo's contention of movement towards the superman and supramental position with every birth also supports this hypothesis.

Should this inter-faith proposition be conceded, nature, rather quality of humans will be determined much more by the values rather than by the amount of information one has mastered. Wisdom that was the prerogative of the saints and seers of all religions is the information and knowledge tested out and purified on the fundamental values. Carrying the argument forward, human beings are essentially value configurations rather than knowledge configuration. Whether a nuclear scientist applies his/her knowledge and expertise in creating a nuclear arsenal or nuclear medicine depends upon his/her value system; knowledge is a mere instrumentality. It is education that provides and strengthens the value aspect of humans to optimise his/her potential.

Nature and Purpose of Education

From the paradigm on the nature of humans portrayed above, the purpose of education becomes comparatively clearer. It is to facilitate the movement of an individual from his/her relative position in the beastliness-divinity continuum. Among the various definitions on the purpose of education, Swami Vivekananda's contention represents the best in this paradigm—"manifestation of the perfection already in man." That 'already in man' (humans) is the divinity, because only the God is perfect and complete. Thus, education leads men and women to their destiny. And, that destiny is the perfection at all levels of living, already in us.

Hence, purpose of education is really to draw out the best in man/woman. While in the conventional education, the 'best' implies optimisation of intellectual capabilities, it means much more from the angle of inter-faith movement. Humans live simultaneously in several planes, namely physical, intellectual, emotional and spiritual. Drawing out the best, from inter-faith strand, implies best in all these planes. Thus a qualified citizen of a global society has to be educated at all planes and not only at the intellectual level.

The International Commisssion on Education for 21st Century in its report to UNESCO *Learning: The Treasure Within* echoed the same sentiments when it delineated living at all the four planes mentioned above and the four pillars of learning, namely, learning to know, learning to do, learning to live together and learning to be. In this paradigm, 'learning to live together' is the key to the safe and habitable 'global society', 'learning to know and learning to do' are the pre-requisites, and 'learning to be' is optimizing the spiritual self within men and women. Educatedness is the process of striving to the holistic development in all the planes.

The qualification for 'educatedness' for the global society, I argue, will be inclusive of the four pillars of learning and beyond. From the angle of education for optimizing total human potential —perfection already in man—educatedness will comprise being:

- Informed
- Skilled
- Cultured
- Emancipated, and
- Self-actualised.

There is a relationship between this set of attributes of educatedness and the four planes of living offering us a matrix structure indicating relevance of each attribute of educatedness for each plane of living, namely, physical, intellectual, emotional and spiritual.

Planes of Living / Attributes of Educatedness	Physical	Mental or Intellectual	Emotional	Psychic or Spiritual
Informed				
Skilled				
Cultured				
Emancipated				
Self-actualised				

The other relationship is among the attributes of educatedness itself. The five attributes are not parallel, these have a hierarchical relationship. These can be placed on a taxonomic structure:

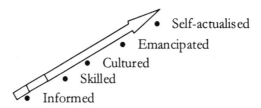

Self-actualised
Emancipated
Cultured
Skilled
Informed

Informed: Every one of us is informed. There are, however, differences; some are informed formally through schools and colleges, some are informed informally. Thus, an informed person may or may not be formally educated in a school. The formally informed individuals through schools and colleges are certified. Indeed, information in this case is standardised around a subject or a group of subjects that are built around a structure of knowledge. In contrast, an 'unqualified' but informed possesses integrated knowledge, may or may not be within any epistemological framework. The difference between a qualified and non-qualified is, thus, on the organisation and structure of knowledge. An unqualified farmer, for example, is informed of farming techniques that draws from biotechnology and farming though he/she may not be familiar with the concerned discipline of science compared to a biotechnologist or an agricultural scientist certified who can differentiate two schools of science.

Although conventionally 'being educated' has been equated with being qualified or 'certified', in the proposed taxonomy of educatedness, *'being informed' is only the lowest level in the hierarchy of educatedness.*

Skilled: The second level in the hierarchy is the ability to do—skills of translating ideas into action. It is the action that not only survives the societies and cultures on the earth but also moves the human civilisation forward. Action is one of the common principles across all religions. Actions are for individual benefit as well as for the benefit of the community. Skills can be physical or motor, intellectual, and emotional skills, and also in combinations of these, like psycho-motor, and social and interpersonal skills. Trained and qualified tradesmen and women as well as rural artisans are skilled. A highly qualified professor in a university is intellectually skilled as much as the otherwise 'so-called unqualified' religious leaders are intellectually skilled. Emotional skills and competence have now caught the imagination of the corporate world, though all religious literatures exhorted human beings to control rather win over anger, sorrow, greed, lust, attachments, etc.

To be educated, an informed person must be skilled too.

Cultured: The third level of educatedness is culturedness. In simpler terms, an educated person must be cultured too. Culture has, metaphorically, been described as the light that emits out of a diamond, and not the diamond itself. In humans, culture represents an individual in his/her totality. It represents the integrated personality that is well rounded, that emits warmth and human values. There are several manifestations of culturedness of an individual. It is manifested by the way an individual treats himself/herself, others, animals, places, objects, and the like. It is the totality of a 'person'. For example, an air-traveller who unhesitatingly litters the spotlessly clean airport with cigarette butts may be informed and skilled on his job, but not cultured. Or, a senior officer in the government throwing files at his subordinates is informed and may be skilled too, but not cultured. Acharya Vinoba Bhave's trio—*Prakriti, Vikriti* and *Sanskriti*[1] represents this concept very well.

---

[1] When a person eats when he/she is hungry, it is *prakriti*; when eats though not hungry (out of greed) is *vikriti*; and when gives food away to another hungry man/woman, suppressing own hunger is *sanskriti*.

Emancipation: One level ahead of culture is emancipation where individuals rise above the artificial boundaries of child grabbing toffies identity & affiliations like religion, caste, creed, gender, linguistic and geographic belonging, social mores, cultural traditions and forms, etc. For example, a male while being proud of being male shall have sense of equality with women and a sense of respect for the female. A Hindu can continue to practise Hindu religion but will have equal respect for Islam, Christianity, Sikhism and other religions of the world. Spiritual leader, Sri Ravi Shankar, in The Millennium Peace Summit of Religious and Spiritual Leaders chaired by Dr. Karan Singh, exhorted that it was not enough to tolerate other religions, one must love other religions. Paramhansa Ramakrishna actually practised more than one religious practice in his own lifetime before he pronounced that 'all roads lead to the same destination' *(jato mat tato path)*. Similarly, a person born in a particular linguistic group can be proud of his/her language and heritage with equal respect and appreciation for the national heritage and diversity of the country and the world. One can simultaneously be a proud national and member of the international community. This is basically achieving freedom from the strangleholds of ignorance, intolerance—*Sa Vidya Ya Vimuktaye* (that is education that liberates).

Thus, in actual terms, educatedness warrants liberation of self from narrow definitions. Information, skills and culture strengthen this process of emancipation.

Self-actualisation: The last and the final level is self-actualisation where emphasis is on achieving the best; optimising the potential in all planes of life, namely, physical, intellectual, emotional and spiritual. In the western tradition, Maslow's Hierarchy of Needs places this at the top of the needs' hierarchy. Vivekananda's definition of purpose of education—'perfection already in man' also indicates to the same direction. Delors' Commission echoed similar proposition when it mentioned that the humans live in physical, intellectual, emotional and spiritual planes. Self-actualisation will imply achieving the best in all the four planes of life.

The purpose of education is to move an individual from the level of information to self-actualisation. Super-imposing these stages with the earlier contention of the purpose of life as movement from beastliness to divinity, it construes that self-actualisation at the top-end merges near around the divinity concept.

Although not from the inter-faith strand, now famous 'four pillars of learning' propagated by the International Commission on Education for 21st Century reverberates the need for comprehensive holistic growth of humans through education. The Commission looked at education as the means for optimizing human potential at physical, intellectual, emotional and spiritual levels. This synthesis of understanding is important to minimise the artificiality of the dialectic contradictions.

Thus, purpose of education is much beyond studying history, economics, mathematics and the like. It is nurturing the seed of immortality already sown in every individual for facile movement from lowest level of being informed to the highest level of self-actualisation. This would also imply that education is the process of developing the wholesomeness of the person where the central core is the values and perceptions, and information and knowledge providing the outer edge for reconstruction of values, and hence his/her socio-spiritual resilience.

Adding the time dimension to this proposition, there are two different implications. Firstly, it signifies movement from informed to self-actualised over time. Secondly, at every age, there is relevance of all the four levels of the taxonomy. Paradigms will be different between a child being informed and an adult. For example, a three year old child pouncing upon the plate of sweets is acceptable culture for his/her age but not when the grown up air traveller pounces on the sweets at the tray forwarded by the airhostess. Understanding, tolerating and appreciating differences between practices in Hindu and Muslim marriage in a village where both the communities live together can be a case of emancipation even at early age. Similarly, one component of self-actualisation will imply efforts to enhance intelligence through due planned positive interventions since according to most schools of psychology, intelligence grows till about 18th year of life.

However, education has to become essentially lifelong process because being informed, skilled, cultured, emancipated and self-actualised has to happen at every stage of life, though self-actualisation at youth is different from actualisation at age.

Conclusion

We had begun our journey with educatedness for global society. A world that is so cleverly crafted with ferociously destructive powers and skills, education is not just the best defence but also the only defence. Education that facilitates realisation of true nature of self, prepares individuals in all facets of their life to optimise their true potential, can only lead to emancipation that is critical to learning to live together.

Present emphasis in education is almost exclusively upon education of the intellect leading to the bare minimum of being informed and somewhat skilled. This is nearer to early generation robots that could process information and act. Education, in the present form hardly touches those softer cores that are so very special of the human species—the values, emotions and spiritual dimensions. Education of the intellect alone is far too inadequate for the global society. Such education can create human beings who are like ships without radars or aircrafts without navigational systems that are well equipped with latest technology and can move fast but unsure of its direction. Educatedness for global society would demand development of humans in all his/her facets.

Inter-faith Education for a
Humane Global Order

Susheela Bhan

Religion has governed human thoughts and action for aeons. An all pervasive force whether consciously realised or unconsciously assimilated, it has guided people's daily lives through canons and precepts such as the ten commandments, the Shariat, laws of Moses, five precepts of Buddhism and others. Individuals and communities have drawn sustenance from religion in times of hardship, emergencies and strife. It has at the same time been a source of law and social control. In all situations, normal or otherwise and for all kinds of people, be it the common folk or the elites, religion has remained central and integral to human life.

Religion and Power

Unfortunately, over time, religion and power have got linked inextricably. Religion's high priests and other power interests have often interpreted religion in narrow terms and in terms of power to control human actions and emotions towards maintaining their hold on the people and preventing changes that could be detrimental to their power interests. These interpretations have been used to inculcate fear and insecurity among the adherents of particular religions and hostility towards other religions to ensure absolute acceptance and obedience. In the process, the inner truth and the fundamental philosophies of religions have been passed over and religious rituals, customs and institutions have been promoted as immutable prescriptions for day-to-day living and attitudes. The power seekers have gone to the extent of dividing people who may have lived in harmony for centuries, to a point that in many parts of the world religious riots and killings have become commonplace and even battles and wars have been fought in the name of religion. From the earliest crusades to the most recent horror of September 11 (2001), a single common causative thread of religious intolerance and hostility runs through them all. In the extreme case of fundamentalists, a deep and abiding hatred of ways of life that are seen as obstacles to the application of stratified, ritualised and doctrinaire religion, they have been indoctrinated to believe in as the only true form of religion, is further ingrained to steel their determination to adopt any means including violence and terrorism to impose the ossified religion on one and all. In such a situation any rational discussion on religion becomes a casuality. Consequently, religion at times gets converted into a mindset as expressed by *Hasan-al-Banna*, founder of Muslim Brethren. "Islam is a faith and ritual, a nation and a nationality, a religion and a state, spirit and deed, holy text and sword" (as Quoted by Mitcheel, 1969). Modern man stands condemned and threatened ominously, by such a mindset which currently combines the military and the missionary dimension with militants from Kashmir to Bosnia or Chechnya, fighting for Islamic rule and re-establishment of a *Khilafat*.

The Conquering Creeds

And yet the problem of religious intolerance is far more basic. It is rooted in the history of the conquering creeds that put on the cloak of religion to kill, enslave and plunder in the name of Jesus or Allah. The rapacious human endeavour was as manifest in the torment and eventual extinction of Europe's Pagans, the crusades, witch-hunts, inquisition and the wars of religion, as it was in the expansionist project of Columbus and his successors which Anatole France described as "the crimes of a whole military and commercial Christianity" (Quoted in Rawino, 2001). Equally rapacious was the Islamic enterprise of relentless destruction and massacres for the glory of Allah. To illustrate, even as the vastness of the Indian sub-continent prevented the Muslim armies from overrunning it (like they had done in respect of countries in the Middle East) and swift conversion proved to be difficult due to antagonistic cultural factors, the first phase of the conquest was marked by premeditated terrorisation, systematic slaughter, forcible circumcision, mass enslavement, destruction of temples and enormous looting. The chronicler of Mahmud of Gazni, the first of Muslim conquerors, who set the pattern, writes of one victory, "Many infidels were slain or taken prisoner, and the Muslims paid no regard to booty until they had satiated themselves with the slaughter of the infidels and the worshippers of sun and fire" (Titus, 1930). This pattern characterised the subsequent muslim invasions too. Wrote Will Durant in her story of civilisation, "The mohemmaden conquest of India is probably the bloodiest story in history. It is a discouraging tale, for its evident moral is that civilisation is a precarious thing whose delicate complex of order and liberty, culture and peace may at any time be overthrown by barbarians invading from without or multiplying within" (Will Durant, 1954).

The Missionary Onslaught

Additionally, there has been the onslaught of Christian missionaries who descended on non-Christian peoples with the absolute claim that Christianity was the sole saviour of mankind, and Christians alone could find salvation. In pursuit of this claim, wherever they went, they created an ethos of persecution, cruelty and conversion by fraud and other unscrupulous methods. In India, this onslaught began with the advent of the Portuguese missionaries who followed the instructions of their king to convert people by 'fire and sword'. While Alphonso Albuquerque destroyed temples and mosques, Francis Zavier brought with him in 1560, the Holy Inquisition to Goa and extended it later to south of Malabar and did not spare even the Syrian Christians. The Protestant Missionaries joined the trade in 1706 and with the Baptist's Semaphore Mission, the clandestine trade shifted to the North in 1793. After the Charter Act of 1813, the missionary activity flourished with evangelisation going to all parts of the country with a special focus on the tribal population. The charity work of education and medical aid remained in the front for the real agenda of conversion. The World Conference of the International Missionary Council held at Tambararm in 1938 noted that evangelism had a central place in all medical and educational institutions. The Report of the Church of Nazarene, made a more firm declaration, "Evangelism is our call. We make no excuse nor ask for any reservation in this period. Jesus has called us to preach the gospel to every creature and we mean to do it in every phase of our work, be it educational, medical or distinctly evangelical. 'Go, teach, win' is the command under which we work. We cannot lessen this emphasis" (*Rashtra Chetna Prakashan*, 1963).

Since the constitution of India provided the right to propagate religion, this was interpreted by the Christian missionaries as their right to convert people as before and with the same strategies. This created serious tensions in many parts of the country. On repeated and persistent protests made to the Govt. of Madhya Pradesh, a 'Christian Missionary Activities Enquiry Committee' under the Chairmanship of Dr. M.B.S. Niyogi, the retired Chief Justice of Nagpur, was set up by the State Government in 1954. The Committee enquired into the missionary activities in the entire tribal heartland of central India and noted that the voluminous oral and documentary evidence before it showed that attacks on Hindu religion, its Gods and deities were an important and integral plank of Christian propaganda. Considering the type of vilification that was going on, it was indisputably clear that such attacks on Hindu religion were at times responsible for breach of peace and public order. The Committee also noted that illegitimate methods such as offering allurements of free education and free medical facilities, money-lending, promoting marriages with Christian girls, adding Christian names to original Indian names, distribution of Christian literature in hospitals, offering prayers in the wards of indoor patients, blessing new-born babies in the name of Jesus, taking sides in litigations or domestic quarrels, kidnapping minor children, abducting women and recruiting labour for plantations in Assam or Andaman as a means of propagating the Christin faith, were used to secure conversions (*Rashtra Chetna Prakashan*, 1963).

The same or similar strategies were used by the missionaries in other countries too. The world-wide highly organised conversion industry is by now a multi-billion dollar business which functions like a trained army to target gullible and vulnerable communities that are innocent of its power and motives. The latest additions to its armory are the most sophisticated communication channels like the websites and radio stations broadcasting in all kinds of languages to the targetted communities of the third world. To cap this all, in December 1999, Pope John Paul II, on a state visit to India, declared in Delhi his mission to plant the "Cross in Asia". In a subsequent declaration 'Dominus Jesus' issued by the Vatican on Aug 6, 2000 and brought to public attention in a press conference on Sept. 5, 2000, the Pope directed the Catholic theologians to obey the scriptural mandate of "baptising all nations".

Islamic onset has not lagged behind. The speed with which the message of Islam has spread, conquering almost one third of the world in less than a century, makes it the fastest growing world religion today. With a population of over 1 billion followers spread over 55 Muslim countries plus those who live in America, west and other non-Islamic countries, Islam has expanded its horizons, thanks to colossal profits from the oil trade, a policy of rapid demographic growth and a steady penetration into the disadvantaged sections of various population groups of the non-Islamic countries. With the latest phase of the talibanisation, it has cut out its most ferocious blood stained path to the front of world's attention as the international community stands shocked and alarmed at what the Islamic gangs, out for blood in the most barbarous style, hold for the future of human civilisation.

Indeed, what the conquering creeds have offered to the pagans, the heathen or the infidel throughout, whether in Europe, the Americas, Africa or Asia is not Jesus' love or Allah's mercy or tolerance but their hegemonic, design, death and devastation, ruins of countless cultures, religious/sectarian geographical divides and bleeding psyches. As early as 1765, Voltaire addressed the Church thus: " You are right, gentlemen, do overrun the earth; it belongs to the strong or the clever who grabs hold of it. You have made the most of the times of ignorance, superstitions, insanity; you have divested us from our heritages, trampled on us; you have grown fat on the substance of the wretched dread, the coming of the day of reason" (Damins, 2001).

It is in this historical context that the current turbulence, violence, disharmony and intolerance has to be examined. If the state of today's world raises serious and troubling questions about the human 'condition and consciousness', 'the day of reason' predicted by Voltaire may have arrived. Today we do not only believe 'that human mind can be controlled and purified, but more importantly, we also know that we have no option but to undertake this exercise before it is too late.

The Non-aggressive Traditions

Here again history shows us the path. Long before the advent of conquering creeds, non-aggressive cultural/religious traditions had flourished on this very earth. Fortunately, these traditions have survived on their own strength. Even as they appear diminished and weakened today, they have retained the core of their non-aggressiveness, their unwillingness to use force, cunning or allurement to plunder or increase their flock. Without unsheathing a sword, the Buddhist monks carried the message of the Buddha far and wide. Red Indians, Africans, Shintiosts and Mesoamericans too have retained their non-aggressive quality. However, the Indian sub-continent has by far been the most significant model of religious tolerance. The story of Indian civilisation and culture is the story of an ocean where waves, currents and cross currents have remained in a state of equilibrium in the midst of new developments, intrusions, movements, adaptations, mutations, disturbances and even storms. Conflicts, contradictions and aggression did not therefore, form the dominant strains of India's diversity of faiths, belief systems and practices, while tolerance, harmony, synthesis and wholeness of life remained integral to its secular cultural growth and development.

How did this unique spectacle come about? The key secular paradigm that informed India's understanding of life—cosmic, human, animal and divine—throughout, was that of *Dharma*. *Dharma* was the universal foundation on which all life was based and the law that sustained life and order. The concept of *dharma* was not secular in the sense of being 'anti-religious, its western connotation, but in the sense that it was all inclusive, universal and eternal. It did not go by any prior assumptions, revelations or scriptures. A rational and empirical analysis of the vast data generated by human experience and understanding in its innumerable and never-ending forms, locales and times, formed the terrain of its theoretical and paraxial parameters. Within this analysis, the central axiom was to seek a balance in which opposites, diversities and many-sided fragments in tension and conflict got integrated into a synergetic whole. The concern was the human condition and not the condition of a particular sect or ethnic group. In its practical application, the *Dharmic* principle, therefore, rejected dualism and treated contradictions and disparities as correlative elements of a total reality. The true identity of the Indian civilisation has thus been strictly *Dharmic*.

It was this all-pervading *Dharmic* consciousness that enabled diverse races and cultures to make India their home. And again, it was this consciousness, which enabled the inhabitants of the sub-continent not only to survive the vicissitudes of time but also to create, develop and nourish a continuous culture. It is true that coming of Muslims to India altered the Indian situation in many fundamental ways. However, over time the *Dharmic* assimilatory process did assert towards a fusion of the two radically different cultures. But by far the Indian encounter with the western civilisation during the last five centuries is a watershed of unparalleled upheaval that the sub-continent has suffered ever in its history. In this upheaval, India began its journey into the western model of religionism, the use of religion as an instrument of hegemony, patronage, power and separatism, the Hindu-Muslim divide and the partition of the country on a religious basis. The consequences have been disastrous in terms of casteism, communalism, fundamentalism, naxalism and so on, leading to numerous forms and styles of turbulence, conflict and violence. Add to this the corrosive and pervasive obsession with material wealth, ritual religiosity and technologic fixation and you have the self-righteous, intolerant man ravaging himself and nature both.

The Crisis of Intolerance

The crisis of intolerance has thus emerged as the central malaise of the human society today and religious fervour and fanaticism as its most poisonous manifestations. On the one hand, humans are suffering from rootlessness, alienation, dehumanisation and insecurity in an age of materialism, mechanisation, aggression and cut-throat competition or consumerism and on the other, majority of the mankind are turning to religion for solace, for strength to cope with the peacelessness within and around them or to fill the gaping void they are living with day in and day out or in desperation to escape the ravages of modernity. Mercifully, some turn to it to understand the meaning and purpose of life and some others to find a way to reach God. Some sort of religious activity has thus become an essential component of the life of the vexed and tormented human psyche.

Unfortunately, an overarching majority of mankind is stuck with the organised and structured religion characterised by exclusivist of the medieval times. Compulsion and perversion in the name of religion not only live on still but in many areas are growing more and more vehement and virulent. Little wonder the turmoil and turbulence in a fast changing, often incomprehensible and sometimes frightening world are on an increase. The bigots make it convenient to trace it to modernisation and call for a reversal to the rigid religious path of good old days. While man in his desperation clings to religion, he is at a dead end with the distorted shape and polluted space of religion around him. Confused, more than ever before, he seeks stability and light at the end of the tunnel.

This then is the biggest challenge to the world leadership. Religion has to be restored to its original place and intent. Religious leaders of all faiths, in particular, have to take the lead in this endeavour. The mangled tenets of religion have to be discarded. A clear distinction between religious rituals, customs and institutions, and its inner truth and most fundamental philosophy has to be established so that this philosophy in its deepest, visionary sense, prevails, and enters the deepest recesses of the human mind to metamorphose human consciousness out of its self-destructive ignorance and the concomitant dehumanisation, hate and violence. Religion could then become the most effective instrument of a transformative process of a fundamental nature with an unlimited reach covering the last man and community. Great religions of the world after all, were basically reform movements in their time. They emerged in specific physical and historical environment as systems of moral/ethical relationships with and within the cosmic order. They brought orderliness and enlightenment to a large mass of the human family. There is no reason why exercised in their full generosity of spirit, they cannot be harnessed to effect the necessary cardinal changes in accordance with modern conditions and needs.

Religion in its full generosity of spirit is a condition of human consciousness. Religious intolerance and hostility reflect the state of our minds and understanding our mind, may, therefore, be crucial to religious harmony. In other words, intolerant or hostile behavior can be traced in part to psychological origins. That is not to deny the role of social, political, economic or historical factors but imply to emphasise the psychological causes that underlie them. This means that current threats to human survival and well being are actually symptoms of our individual, or collective psychological dysfunctions including ignorance, misunderstanding/lack of understanding, misinterpretation, indoctrination, attitudinal perversities and the like. The most important question of our time, therefore, is this: how can we create a mental state which will help us to understand world problems, our role in creating them and further mobilise and empower us to correct them and even learn individually and collectively, as we do so? The crucial requirement then saw teaching/learning process targeted both at the conscious and unconscious levels, a process of individual and social evolution speeded up by the wakening of a new consciousness that will efface the distortions of the unconscious as well. This is what inter-faith education is all about.

Inter-faith Education

Is such an educational process possible in a world of organised religious intolerance? Such an educational process, I would like to submit, is not only possible but also necessary. Because it is not enough to accept or emphasise that religious intolerance, hatred and violence stem from a lack of genuine understanding of and empathy towards religious traditions other then our own and as such we should develop such an understanding and empathy through inter-faith education. The real challenge, in fact, is to delineate the parameters of such an educational exercise both in conceptual and methodological terms and that in my view is a difficult task, rendered even more difficult on account of the serious limitations that an inter-faith educator faces.

The first such limitation is the problem of right understanding of religious traditions. In the western model of religious understanding, the knowledge of another's faith is sought by academics in the objective and scientific study of religions. They comprehend religious texts and translate these, write treatises on the origin and history of religions, identify various denominations or sects and analyse religious practices. However, such endeavors may make for intellectual accomplishments, they do not help the scholar to appreciate or experience the beauty or truth of a religion, the peace of mind and spirit through religious experience or the balance and strength that faith generates. Understanding religion is not the same thing as understanding economics, sociology or physics. Religions provide frameworks within which the transformation of human existence from self-centeredness to Reality-centeredness can take place. These frameworks are not dry scientific statements but complex mixtures of the mythical, the symbolic, the philosophical and the empirical that provide freedom for a large variety of human perceptions of the Real. And each of these perceptions is valid. Real interreligious understanding therefore, has to go beyond the intellectual approach. It will come only when a person has the capacity to understand his own religion, delve deep into the conflicts within him as also their causes and to rise above his ego-bound perceptions and viewpoint. An inter-faith education in particular, cannot treat his religion as an island, above and separate from others but only as one of the valid paths to salvation/liberation among many others. On the other hand, he will gain a larger understanding of his own religion in encountering and accepting the numerous ways in which the major cultural streams have enabled human beings to attain consciousness of the Real in distinctly different ways. Only then can he acquire a genuine and his own understanding of religious paths that are different from empathetic and stand transformed in the recognition of the truth and beauty of each religious tradition. "If we are to accept other religions as we would have them respect our own", said Gandhi, "a friendly study of the world religions is a sacred duty".

This brings us to the prime proposition that the multiplicity of religious forms and methods of worship are features of a divine unity and this unity in diversity is the manifestation and recognition of the spiritual nature of all living things. Spiritual consciousness, the sacred core of every individual irrespective of his religion, holds life as a unified entity. Ramana Maharshi says, " O God, each sect or religion, each creature is a different pearl and you are the thread that invisibly runs through each of them" (Sri Arunachala Astakam 01. 4). What does this imply for the inter-faith educator? That even as different paths to salvation exist and must flourish, religion has to be elevated to the spiritual contemplative plane towards a quest for perfection. That the extermination of the affectivity and beauty of the variety of beliefs is violence against the soul. Symbiosis among all the paths alone will provide a better understanding of the Self and the transcendental. The very quintessence of the right to religion is spiritual evolution. To quote Dr. Karan Singh, "Immeasurable brilliance of the Divine cannot be imprisoned within any one creed or doctrine. The golden thread of spiritual realisation that weaves together all the great religious traditions of the world need to be strengthened, so that as we enter the new millennium, we can shed the baggage of fanaticism, fundamentalism and bigotry that cruelly disturbed the twentieth century". Indeed, the inter-faith educator has the responsibility to promote religious and spiritual quests that not only know no boundaries, but also make no room for denigrating or despising other religions or elements to indoctrinate, convert or discriminate. In doing so, he will generate the true inter-faith dialogue, a dialogue based on 'mutual respect, equality, interdependence and understanding of the true nature and destiny of man.'

A Dialogical Process

In our discourse on inter-faith education, the term dialogue is in vogue currently. We are in fact, living in an age of dialogue. It refers to an educational process of a conversation between two or more religions. However, an inter-religious dialogue is no ordinary dialogue, no supermarket of ideas. Its character and complexion in terms of its conceptual frame, its objectives, its content methodologies, the educational environment or the expected outcomes are very special. Inter-religious dialogue involves communication, mutual participation, sharing of religious experience, and reciprocity of response, interaction and interrelationship. The objective is to bring about a deeper knowledge, understanding and acceptance of different religious perspectives towards a shared pursuit of the ultimate destiny of man. The dialogue may not require a formal discussion or a colloquy. It may be spoken or a written exchange or just a communication in silence and presence. Because dialogue here does not restrict itself to an understanding of doctrines at an intellectual level nor an exposition of theological concepts narrowly defined religious topics. It is rather, sharing experience that covers attitudes, values, convictions, ideological persuasions, religious outlook *vis-à-vis* the problems of life, matters of faith, devotion, togetherness propinquity and communion, or religious experience and builds living enriching, and transformative relationships between dignified and equal partners who discover and encounter each other as partners in a common quest. Building such relationships is the core of inter-religious dialogue. The essential element is 'seeing the other' or 'experiencing in the other' in term of the 'I-thou' relationship of Martin Buber, who talks of original togetherness of persons in the same human nature.

The Components of a Socialisation Model

The objective of achieving such intense levels of humanism is a tall order. How does the inter-faith education use the instrumentality of education to generate a process of socialisation that can inculcate ideas, beliefs, values, experiences and behaviours conducive to the quality of religious harmony suggested in religious diversity? The approach obviously will vary with different religious/cultural contexts and locales. However, the basic framework will have a general validity. It will form a guideline for the construction of any number of modules appropriate to specific situations. The framework will reflect the learning goals, the curriculum and strategies for operationalzing the educational process. While an extensive listing of learning goals is neither possible nor feasible, the following suggested outline indicate a basis for further discussion and elaboration.

Learning Goals

1. To gain an unbiased knowledge of and reverence for different religions, an appreciation of their essential tenets and an understanding of different religious paths as pathways to spiritual evolution of the human mind.

2. To learn that a humane world order cannot be established without an adherence to the common teachings of all religions such as the imperative of an ethical order, the detachment and the ascetic orientation it demands, the transcendence and intimacy of the absolute, the obedience due to the Divine will, the law of non-violence and the sacredness of the physical universe.

3. To learn that above-mentioned precept gets manifested in and as such command adherence to ideals of justice, liberty, equality and fraternity enshrined in our constitution.

4. To learn about the lives of great men of religion, dead and alive who enlightened men, groups and whole societies, irrespective of their religious affiliation.

5. To learn to dismantle narrow loyalities and develop loyalities to the human brotherhood through tolerance, creativity, compassion, empathy, sharing, cooperation and love.

6. To learn that no religious situation is a given unalterable phenomenon. Religions as well as individual thinking and action are socially mediated.

7. To learn that even as individual freedom of action is limited by society, he can expand it and use it for religious change and reform in solidarity with others.

8. To learn that religious harmony is in the interest of adherents of all religions and religious intolerance is promoted by power interests.

9. To develop a sense of responsibility for mobilizing groups and movements to fight the status quo and resolving conflicts through non-violent techniques of conflict resolution.

10. To develop critical thinking to analyse situations of religious conflict, its reasons and impact on the groups involved.

11. To learn to recognise one's own prejudices which are socially conditioned and which distort perceptions and limit the freedom of thinking and action.

The Learning Process

The learning process will constitute cognitive construction, learning through reinforcement, social modeling and religious/spiritual bonding. Cognitive construction will pertain to assembling data from the perceived world and relating it to data already stored in the mind of the learner. Through the educational experience the learner will not merely incorporate readymade data but rediscover and reexamine it to be able to discard data and images that have no authenticity. Classical Buddhist psychology offers insights here. It traces the problem of the distorted images of the world and ourselves, which we perceive to be correct, to three basic causes—greed, hatred and delusion. The eastern psychologists also locate the shaping and fixation of the distorted images in dualistic ways of thinking and seeing, that is looking at the world in term of opposite, good and bad, us and them, thereby missing the commonality and unity that underlie them and comprehending them as competing entities instead of the entity of one humankind.

The inter-faith educator must, therefore, pull the learners to reflect on the distorted images, recognise the errors in their ways of thinking and perceiving and awaken them to correct defenselessly and honestly the distorted images, in order to accelerate their individual and collective maturation. One has to note also that cognitive maturation and emotional maturation are interlinked and any inter-faith educational experience must take both into account.

Selective reinforcement of responses will aim at behavioural modification and redirection. Certain reinforcements previously acquired in respect of a sequence of behaviours, may be withdrawn and new ones created for a more desirable behaviour pattern. Modelling can be used through observation from a distance. It may take the form of watching visuals on the TV, Films, Documentaries or other features or reading life stories of prophets, saints or stories/comics that draw attention to or nurture a set of values, attitudes and beliefs.

Cultural/religious and spiritual bonding will nurture a deep understanding, harmony, communion, compassion, love, peace and altruism. At the social and religious/cultural levels, bonding will involve sympathetic, supportive, nurturing and aiding attitudes and behaviour in recognition of both ritual and non-ritual dimensions of the cultural/religious life of individuals and groups. Secondly, the inter-faith educator will in his socialisation model incorporate a spiritual-intuitive bonding process. This will focus on the divine human covenant in seeking the beneficence of divine wisdom that is not subject to the inadequacy and fallibility of human understanding. Spiritual bonding which can be termed as divine human bonding will aim at reordering, reconstructing and transmuting human identities, selves and relationships, not with reference to social/cultural/religious covenants but, with reference to a trans-specific encounter with the omnipotent and omnipresent Reality of the cosmic order. Methodology here would constitute meditation sessions, Yoga sessions or communion in prayer or silence and sharing of spatula experiences, toward the realisation of the fundamental unity and oneness of man (for fuller discussion, refer Boulding, 1979).

The entire process will promote confidence in self, ability to solve problems and cope with stress, optimism about the future, emotional warmth, feelings of responsibility for the well-being of others and sensitivity to and sympathy with suffering individuals. The participant-learners will acquire new knowledge, values and skills, and develop cognitive, emotional, intuitive and spiritual capacities. Simultaneously he will get exposed to beliefs, opinions, values and attitudes that will predispose him to sharing, cooperation, bonding, altruism, and making constructive changes in the environment around.

Educational Spaces

Inter-faith education will have to cover all age groups, children, youth, adults, and the old. The learning modules will naturally differ with distinct requirements of a particular group. The educator can make use of five categories of spaces, *viz.* the family, the neighbourhood, formal and non-formal educational institutions, other institutional settings and the mass media. The convenience and the availability of the participant-learners, will determine the timing and frequency of the educational exercise. Regular courses of varied durations can and should be organised in collaboration with organisations such as the scouts, girl guide's, NSS, NCC, youth clubs/kendras, students' unions, the parent-teacher associations and the like. Philanthropic organisation like Rotary Clubs, Lions Club, Women's Organisations including religious and professional organisations should be motivated to join the inter-faith education movement. Visits to famous shrines, temples, mosques, churches and ashrams should be organised as inputs into inter-faith education. So should the celebration of religious festivals be used for the purpose.

The Curricular Directions

The curricula prescribed for courses in educational institutions at different levels should be restructured to incorporate inter-faith education and to introduce the students to common messages that emanate from different religious traditions. For participant-learners outside the educational institutions, foundation courses and other need-based courses will have to be developed by experts. An unbiased treatment of religions and their emphasis on the moral and spiritual uplift of man should remain a major focus. These messages can further be carried to the community through extension education services available in most of the educational institutions, particularly the agricultural colleges and universities, teacher training institutions, departments of adult education, women's studies centers at the universities and so on. Additionally, inter-faith education may be organised in educational institutions with a wide membership of willing and interested students who can organise activities including lectures, film shows, seminars, symposia, workshops, discussion groups, with the guidance of the members of the Faculty. Organizing public meetings, including corner meetings or street plays, should also go a long way in bringing about public on inter-faith issues. Finally, a networking of all inter-faith education centers will give a momentum to the development of an inter-faith education movement, enrich the effort, and enable the participant educators and learners to share experiences and resources.

A Council for Inter-faith Research, Education and Communication

The above discussion makes a case for an inter-faith education movement as a transformative struggle of a fundamental nature. Thinking of inter-faith education as an impulsive response to the attacks of fundamentalists, or religious riots is not the answer. A conscious, mature and enduring exercise with clear cut goals, strategies for the short run as well as a long-term perspective with solid linkages ranging from the local, sub-national, national to international levels is the need of the hour. Religion is a resource integral to every individual life, east or west. It has the highest potential for metamorphosing the human mind and psyche from an aggressive entity into a humane entity at peace with himself and the world around him. It is the individual's route to moral stature and beyond that to his self-realisation.

The task of developing the conceptual and paraxial parameters of inter-faith education is formidable. We have not begun even the initial spadework in this direction. We are naturally not equipped to undertake the gigantic task with any confidence or competence. While the mainstream social science does not even recognise the necessity or the value of a transformative religious movement, the educational experts and religious leaders are inhibited by the constitutional credo of secularism, which forbids any kind of religious instruction in an educational institution funded by the state. However, if we are seriously convinced and committed to the idea and its effective implementation, a necessary step would be to set up an Indian council of Inter-faith Research, Education and Communication, aided by the State if possible/feasible or funded by public secular/religious agencies. Under the auspices of the council, Centres for inter-faith Education Studies could also be set up in each region and in due course in each state. Such a facility would provide the inter-faith education movement, the necessary back up in terms of research, theoretical frameworks, training modules for educators and the learners, methodologies, educational materials, and other pedagogic prerequisites. In due course, the experts working at the said institutions could generate a body of knowledge that would guide the course of the movement and sustain it on an enduring basis.

One would also like to suggest that the Temple of Understanding and other organisations that are currently involved in building an inter-faith education movement, should lobby for the establishment of an 'Inter-faith Academy' under the auspices of the United Nations. This would not only bring about the necessary recognition and commitment to the movement, but lead the member-states to develop policies and programmes suited to the specific requirement of each nation as an integral part of their educational, developmental projects.

Towards an Authentic Humane Global Order

We have discovered to our cost that our civilisation today, informed by the European Enlightenment, the materialistic interpretation of science, technology and progress, and the concept of secularisation has landed us in the grip of a multidimensional crisis (Kothari, 1988). So deep is our insecurity and fragmentation, and so powerful and deadly are our armaments that the question of the very survival of our civilisation, of the species, the survival of the entire creation, stares us in the face. We seem to be in the throes of a breakdown already, economically, politically, socially, culturally, ecologically, intellectually and psychologically. As we try to examine and comprehend our deeply divided world characterised by inequity and exploitation, aggression, violence and wars, a wholesale normative vacuum, and the seductive ethic of lavish life styles, we recognise that we have to reconceptualise the problematique of a human world order before destructive forces released devour irretrievably. An Inter-faith education movement would be one of the most significant purposive interventions, in this regard. In this enterprise of utmost urgency we have to go back to the humane paradigms of the ancient Indians, Chinese or the Greeks, that did not treat knowledge as an instrument of domination and power, but as a liberator of the human spirit. That is what enabled the '*Dharmic*' worldview of the ancient Indians to live by an awareness of limits and balance, discrimination between knowledge and understanding, knowledge and character, and knowledge and wisdom. If our projects of modernity and post-modernity have failed because of the lack of the imperative of a normative framework, let this vacuum be filled by the absolute ethical standards inherent in all religions. This alternative, crying for attention, is the most promising route to an authentic humane world order. And an inter-faith education movement is a decisive and potent instrument to usher in a mindset that will actualise and give substance to the vision of such aft global order.

References

1. Hasan-al-Banna, al-Mu'tammar al-khamis Quoted in Richard P. MitceII, *The Society of the Muslim Brethren*, London: Oxford University Press, 1969, p.233.

2. Anatole France, Sur la pierre blanche ("On the White Stone", Paris, CaIman-Levy, 1928, p. 163, written in 1905) Quoted in Michel

Danino, *The Conqueror and The Conquered*, paper presented at World Congress for the Preservation of Religious Diversity held in New Delhi on Nov. 15-17, 2001.

3. Murray T, Titus, *Indian Islam: A Religious History of Islam in India*, New York: Oxford University Press, 1930.

4. Will Durant, *The Story of Civilisation, Part I, Our Oriental Heritage*, New York: Simon and Schuster, 1954, p.495.

5. Quoted in *"A summary of the Christian Missionary Activities Enquiry Committee, Madhya Pradesh*, 1963, Rashtra Chetna Prakashan and Charitable Trust, 1963.

6. *Ibid.* p.3

7. Voltaire, Dictionnaire Philosophique ("Philosophical Dictionary"), Paris, G7- Flammarion, 1964, p.459, Quoted in Michel Danino Op. Cit.

8. Chinweizu, *The West and the Rest of Us: White Predators, Black Slavers and African Elite*, Vintage, 1975, p.3

9. Chaturvedi, B. *Dharma, India and the World Order*, Edinburgh: Saint Andrew Press, 1993.

10. For a fuller discussion please see, Boulding, Elise, 'The Child and Non-violent Social Change' in Christoph Wulf (Ed). *Handbook on Peace Education*, Frankfurt: International Peace Research Association, 1974, pp.116-124.

11. Rajni Kothari, *Transformation and Survival: In Search, of a Humane World Order*, Delhi: Ajanta Publications, 1988

Gandhian Perspective on Education

K.D.Gangrade

A cartoonist had tellingly related story of the level of moral degeneration in Indian and other countries. The first one says: "On closer examination, they have found the charges of corruption, defalcation and moral turpitude against me, were all acts of utmost honesty." The second says, "We know that unscrupulous opposition fellows, to gain political mileage, will exploit our corrupt practices, misuse of power, and undemocratic methods". The causes attributed to such a pathological situation are diverse. The often mentioned causes are a defective educational system which does not emphasise moral values, failure to prepare and equip students for economic pursuit and life at large; lack of sufficient and healthy contacts between students and teachers, and exploitation and misleading of citizens by political parties and politicians. Some people feel that the social maladies of the day are symptoms of wide spread problem of social indiscipline which get manifested in phenomena like corruption, bribery, nepotism and political opportunism and generally immoral behaviour.

The present day processes of political manoeuvre and the implementation of development schemes are acting as catalysts of a collective decadence. A society which lays greater emphasis on the accumulation of power and wealth than on morality, learning and humane behaviour, and places more faith in demagogy rather than on the shared endeavours for understanding and participation in the process of change and development, is bound to pay a heavy price for its lack of collective wisdom.

The continuance of widespread violence and unrest show a general decadence of higher moral and ethical values. The lack of fellow feeling, trust, faith and concerns superceding personal and group loyalties is suggestive of the fact that the tried and tested path of tolerance, justice, morality, and trusteeship illumined by the leaders of yesteryears, specially Gandhiji, has been generally forsaken by the present leaders. Gandhi had assumed that once people are awakened, they would become a revolutionary force. They would explode if their minimum expectations are not satisfied. This explosion could take many unpleasant and ugly forms. Careful and systematic consideration of alternatives suggests that in order to come out of the present malaise, the only remedy lies in adapting to or adopting the Gandhian path of education.

An imaginative tailor had put up two hoardings. The first says, "God has created you women and men". The second says, "We make you Ladies and Gentlemen". This is the primary aim of education. It should prepare citizens of the global society to consider whole world as one family.

Meaning of Education

The ordinary meaning of education is a knowledge of letters. To teach boys and girls reading, writing and arithmetic is called primary education. A peasant earns his bread honestly. He has everyday knowledge of the world. He knows fairly well as to how he should behave towards his parents, his wife, his children and his fellow villagers. He understands and observes the rules of morality. But, sometimes he cannot write his own name. Will you add an inch to his happiness by equipping him with education? Do you wish to make him discontented with his cottage or his lot? And even if you want to do that, he will not need such an education. Carried away by the flood of western thought, we come to the conclusion that without weighing pros and cons, we should give this kind of education to the people. Gandhi's emphasis was on three Hs— Head, Heart and Hand.

Gandhi in Hind Swaraj had defined education thus: "That man I think has had a liberal education who has been so trained in youth that his body is the ready servant of his will and does with ease and pleasure all the work that as a mechanism it is capable of; whose intellect is a clear, cold, logic engine with all its parts of equal strength and in smooth working order; whose mind is stored with a knowledge of the fundamental truths of nature... whose passions are trained to come to heel by vigorous will, the servant of a tender conscience... who has learnt to hate all villains and to respect others as himself. Such a one and no other, I conceive, has had a liberal education, for he is in harmony with nature. He will make the best of her and she of him". This is true education. Gandhi emphatically says that the sciences such as Geography, Astronomy, Algebra, Geometry, etc. have never been able to help him in controlling his senses. Therefore, whether you take elementary education or higher education, it is not required for the main thing. It does not make men of us. It does not enable us to do our duty. Gandhi further says that he has not run down a knowledge of letters in all circumstances. All he has shown is that we must not make a fetish of it. It is not our *Kamadhuk* (fulfillment of desires). As an ornament it is likely to sit well on us, it now follows that it is not necessary to make this education compulsory. Our ancient school system is enough. Character building has the first place in it and that is primary education. A building erected on that founding will last.

Gandhi's educational ideas are best understood and appreciated in the framework of his total philosophy of which the two cardinal principles were: (I) Truth, and (2) Non-violence. There are at least three categories into which Gandhian notions may be classified. They are, simply stated: Gandhian objectives, Gandhian principles and Gandhian means. The overall objective for Gandhi were two: *Swaraj* and *Sarvodaya*. Prominent among his principles were non-violence or *ahimsa*, adherence to truth and dignity of labour. Finally, Gandhian means included not only *Satyagraha* as the most important technique but also a new system of education. Gandhi advocated transformation of men and women, and for this transformation, one of his important tools was education.

The ultimate aim of Gandhian education was to create a *satyagrahi*, a truthful and non-violent person. Truth, non-violence, service to humanity and fearlessness were the goals, and education was the means of these. Character building was the most important function of education. Education was to develop skills in living and working, and draw the best out of each individual. In a letter to his son Manilal written from Volksrust prison in 1909, he said, "...education does not mean a knowledge of letters but it means character building". He distinguished between literacy and knowledge, and held that literacy in itself was no education.

Development of human personality was far more significant than the accumulation of intellectual tools and knowledge. He envisioned the acquisition of true education primarily through participation in a particular pattern of life in a community and not merely through formal instruction in schools. Schools were to prepare citizens of a new global society—a non-violent society and teach children to live on the basis of co-operation, truth and *ahimsa*. The essential tenets of the system of education as propounded by Gandhi can be summed up as follows:

1. Education must serve the nation's and global society's needs, consistent with the philosophy of freedom, truth and non-violence;

2. It must promote equality of all religions, and of all women and men;

3. It should give equal importance to intellectual training and manual work which should be socially useful and productive;

4. Mother tongue should be the medium of instruction at all levels; and

5. The curricula and other arrangements should aim at serving the needs of people.

Character building has been emphasised by Swami Vivekananda and other saints of India such as Sri Aurobindo, Sri Ramakrishna Pararmhans, and so on. Wearing saffron robe with turban on head, a staff in hand and shawl on his shoulders, Swami Vivekananda was roaming on the roads of Chicago. This attire of Vivekananda was a thing of wonder meant for the Americans. A lady, who was following Swami Vivekananda, said to her mate, "See the man wearing this ludicrous dress". Swamiji immediately understood that these

Americans were ridiculing his Indians dress. He stopped a while and addressed the lady, "Sister, don't be surprised at my dress. In your country, the dress of a person is the measure of gentlemanliness, but in the country from which I have come, we judge a person from his character and not apparel.

Vinoba, when he was asked about Gandhi said, "Science plus spiritual knowledge is equal to Gandhi [S+S=G]." An American friend (*Patricia*) who joined Vinobaji's Ashram was with him in the long *Padyatra*. Once Nirmala Deshpande (Vinoba's disciple) told Patricia, "You ought to have been born in India. You are more Indian than many of us." The reply she gave can never be forgotten. She said, "It is good that I was born in America, I now look to India. If I were born in India, I would have looked to America."

Let me state an interesting story told by an American friend. A group of American farmers had gone to New York and stayed in a posh hotel. The hotel room was on the 80th floor. Then all of them went for shopping. When they came back carrying gift loads of different things, they found that the lift was not working. They decided: "We will climb the stairs and each one will tell us his own tale of woe while climbing the stairs". That way they climbed 79 stairs. When the turn of the last man came, he hesitated a little. Others asked him. "Why do you hesitate? Your tale of woe is also our tale of woe and we will share it". He said:. "You people were kind enough to entrust me with the key of our room when we went out. Now, while climbing the 80th floor, I realised that I have forgotten the key on the ground floor."

After all, we are becoming space men and space women. Let us advance the progress so far as science and technology are concerned. But let us not forget the key of spiritual or moral progress on the ground floor.

Similar sentiments were expressed in a letter written by Abraham Lincoln to the Head Master of the school in which his son was studying. He wrote among other things, "In school, teach him that it is far more honourable to fail than to cheat. Teach him to have faith in his own ideas, even if everyone tells him that they are wrong. Try to give him the strength not to follow the crowd when every one is getting on the bandwagon. Teach him to listen to all men, but teach him also to filter all he hears on a screen of truth, and take only the good that comes through. Teach him how to laugh when he is sad. Teach him there is no shame in tears. Teach him to close his ears to howling mob, and to stand and fight if he thinks he is right. Treat him gently, but do not cuddle him, because only the test of fire makes fine steel. Let him have the courage to be impatient, let him have the patience to be brave. Teach him always to have sublime faith in himself too because then he will always have faith in mankind and global society. Then only he will become a true citizen of global society."

Now that is what we have to learn for value-oriented education, and here there is a hint about methodology, which involves people sympathising with one another. Actually, it does not stop at mere sympathy. It required complete identification or empathy and these in my views, are teachings of Gandhiji.

Developing Body, Mind and Spirit

Man is made of three constituents—the body, mind and spirit. The knowledge that is being imparted today may possibly develop the mind a little, but certainly does not develop the body and spirit. Gandhiji had a doubt about the development of the mind too, because it does not mean that the mind has developed if we have filled it with a lot of information. We cannot therefore say that we have educated our mind. A well-educated mind serves man in the desired manner. Our literate mind of today pulls us hither and thither. That is what a wild horse does. Only when a wild horse is bridled, we can we call it a trained horse. How many 'educated' young man of today are so trained?

Now let us examine body. Are we supposed to cultivate the body by playing tennis, football or cricket for an hour every day? It does certainly build up the body. Like a wild horse, however, the body will be strong but not trained. A trained body is healthy, vigorous and sinewy. The hand and feet can do any desired work. A pick-axe, a shovel, a hammer, etc. are all like ornaments to a trained hand and it can wield them. The hand can ply the spinning wheel well as also the ring and the comb while the feet work on the loom. A well-trained body does not get tired in trudging 30 miles. It can scale mountains without getting breathless. Do the students acquire such physical culture? We can assert that modern curricula do not impart physical education in this sense.

The less said about the spirit the better. Only a seer or a seeker can enlighten the soul. Who will awaken the dormant spiritual energy in us all? Teachers can be had through an advertisement. Is there a column for spiritual quest in the testimonials which they have to produce? Even if there is one, what is its value? How can we get through advertisements, teachers who are seekers after self-realisation? And education without enlightenment is like a wall without a foundation or, to employ an English saying like a whited sepulcher. Inside there is only corpse eaten up or being eaten up by insects (See Navajivan Education Supplements, 28 February, 1926, CW 30, pp 58-59).

Influence of Education

Much of the power and influence, which is attributed to education, is derived essentially from agencies imparting informal education, such as the family, the peer group, sometimes organised as a youth movement, and the mass media. The relative strengths of the educational influences of formal and informal education vary from period to period and from country to country. It is assumed that the formal education system is in a position to act as the central coordinating link between all other educational influences. It also appears more easily and obviously capable of modification in the light of social goals.

It has been widely suggested that in India, in recent years, the formal system of education has been failing in its effectiveness as the central educational influence. The other influences like the political movement have historically played an important role in Indian national life. To this extent, education has not had certain roles commonly associated with it, for example formation of higher values. Since Independence a common national political movement no longer seems to be operative.

Manpower

The effectiveness of formal education depends to a great extent on the quality of manpower, specially teachers.

Types of Teachers

There are four types of teachers. The first is a mediocre teacher who tells. The second is a good teacher who explains. The third is a superior teacher who demonstrates. The fourth is a great teacher who inspires. There is dearth of teachers belonging to the last category.

The teaching profession does not attract bright young people anymore at least at the school leaving stage. We celebrate every 5th September as Teacher's day. Let us have a bit of self-analysis.

In the primary school they (students) worship you or fear you. In the middle school, they admire you or ridicule you behind your back. In the senior school they assess you. Whatever they do, they can never be indifferent to you because you have become an inescapable part of their lives.

One of the greatest rewards of teachings is that you can actually see personalities develop.

Job Satisfaction

In a study it was found that less than 20-25 percent teachers really love to teach. It is not enough to place emphasis on the quality of teaching but one has to seriously consider job satisfaction as a key factor as well.

Dissatisfaction leads to sub-standard performance, thus the problem of the quality of teachers arises. It may be true that most of the capable personnel have left the profession to find "greener pastures" elsewhere. In this age when education is a necessary acquisition in a game of survival, teachers are falling behind. Instead of offering knowledge or becoming positive role models, many teachers are busy taking care only of their personal interests.

Prestigious Occupation

Teaching is considered a prestigious and a noble profession. But many teachers have realised that nobody can survive on prestige alone. If teachers could spend less time worrying about their own existence, they would be able to spend more time preparing their lesson plans. The teacher's emoluments in recent years have considerably improved.

Respect of Teachers

In the past, teachers were most respected, second only to parents. In the traditional social systems, money was not important because our traditional economy was rather comfortable to live with. Teachers were not highly paid. But then food and the cost of living were low. Even with their small salary they lived quite happily and comfortably.

It all started after the Second World War when consumerism entered our society. In that society, so called 'development' was a new concept then. 'Development' was taken by many to mean that people had to import and follow foreign values. Today's consumer-oriented society breeds unlimited greed and people accept it unquestioningly.

Teachers have steadily been losing ground as members of a formerly influential group. This is true specially of the last couple of years which have seen the mass media wielding greater influence than ever before. Now, like everybody else, teachers are influenced by the media. They also need to try this product or that which they too have seen in advertisements. This is the reason why people are always hungry for money. The once prestigious teaching profession has become a lowly occupation because it does not yield high pay.

Society is becoming more complicated every day. Materialism has become an integral part of modern life. It is not just teachers who have declining moral standards, the whole society is faced with this problem.

Lack of Motivation

Society criticises teachers for not living up to its expectations. People are quick to find faults with teachers and blame them for not able to keep up with the changes that are occurring in the world. They take teachers to task for virtually all the problems affecting our society. One explanation for lack of competence of teachers is that they lack motivation. Low pay, unfavourable working conditions and poor prospects of career advancement keep teachers in mental lethargy.

Today people in the teaching profession are looked down upon, as people with low pay and no future. This is particularly true of the rural schools. Leaving teachers to be solely responsible for developing youth is a bit cruel. Every section of society should be contributing to this basic task. Parents should, in fact, be the first people to watch over and help to educate their children.

It must be realised that teaching is a meaningful occupation, not the last choice. The priority in education should be to harmonise people, not just to emphasise the mundane subject of ways to make money.

Conclusion

Despite many deficiencies the present education has not reached out to all. Teacher is the key to education.If we are seeking a change in the education system, let us begin with the primary source—the teacher. The first step is to approach the needs of our teacher more systematically. Let us institutionalise the development of our teachers and establish programmes that train and equip them the way we train engineers and doctors. Let us teach ourselves the needs of the teaching- learning profession and understand that they require our special attention. Let us do this for our teachers, our children and future generations.

In a world dominated by technology, enhancing the quality of education is the key to future. It is only through knowledge and learning that we can become competitive, improve productivity, and strengthen our work culture. Technology provides opportunities as well, particularly in reaching out to masses and in creating greater awareness. The teaching professional must rise to these challenges.

It is not over simplification to stress that the need of the day is to produce" good global citizen". Today, when India confronts diverse challenges of change and advancement, it is imperative that we profuse a generation of good men and women. In our efforts to widen consciousness of responsibilities and awareness of rights and duties, teachers can truly make the difference. The teachers could be a powerful means to spread the message of sharing and caring of a willingness to sacrifice and of a commitment to the larger good.

Human resources are indisputably our great assets and it is only through their development that India can progress. Our vision of growth is accompanied by social justice. We believe in secularism and pluralism as the basic tenets of our national ethos. The achievements of teachers were and are evaluated by the conduct and capabilities of the students.

To sum up, destiny of future India and global society is being shaped in its educational institutions. And in this effort teachers were and are the critical "input". The morals of a civil global society are like its teeth. The more decayed they are, the more it hurts to touch them. The horrific attack on Tuesday, the 11th September 2001, speaks that man has completely lost balance of his mind. This inhuman act is essentially an attack on the very heart of humanity itself. The remedy to prevent such tragedies and to salvage society, we need Gandhian education system, which gives equal emphasis and importance to body, mind and spirit.

Let me conclude by quoting from the final address of Swami Vivekananda (27th Sept 1893). In spite of resistance, 'Help and not Fight', 'Assimilation and not Destruction', 'Harmony and Peace and not Dissension.' These are the fundamental principles to develop citizens of global society to lead a peaceful and harmonious life. Unfortunately, nationalism and religions taught by politicians and priests have been the reason behind most of the wars in history The human terrorist attack on America recently has its roots in the same teachings and indoctrination. People have been taught too much of patriotism and devotion to their religions that they have lost their individuality and sensitivity and have become suicidal slaves to ideologies. The root cause of all violence and terrorism is in the thinking—the flawed ideologies that he or she has always been taught. These bind him to the chains of actions that are unjustifiable and abhorred in a civilised society.

Gandhian Education is the freedom to become a human being, with consciousness above instincts, caste and colour, nations and religions, and recognises others as human beings too. This universal love alone will enable to build a global civilised society. Gandhian concept of education will infuse a new spirit into present education system. Changes are brought about gently, almost imperceptibly and without doing violence to values of Truth and Non-violence, which all people cherish. Every person must understand that whatever intelligence, bodily strength, and wealth he possesses is his for the welfare of all. This is genuine Sarvodaya. This can be fostered by education. In fact, a social order based on mutual trust implies that the varied capacities of all its members are wisely encouraged and used immensely to build a non-violent global society.

References

1. Laxman, *Cartoons*, The Times of India, 14 and 15 May, 1993, New Delhi.See Gangrade K.D.'s article *Moral Integration: A Plea for Peaceful Society* Gandhi Marg, Vol.XIV.No2, July-Sept. 1994

2. Gangrade, K.D. *Moral Integration: A Plea for Peaceful Society*, Gandhi Marg, Vol.XIV, No.2 July-Sept. 1994

3. Gandhi, M.K. *Hindi Swaraj*, Navajivan Publishing House, Ahmebabad, 1989. pp.77-78

4. *Ibid*, p. 71

5. *Ibid*, p. 80

6. *Ibid*, p. 82

7. Basu, Aparna: Gandhi on Education, *In Gandhian Perspective of Nation Building for World Peace*, (Ed) N.Radhakrishnan, Konark Publishers Pvt. Ltd., New Delhi 1992, pp 101-107, specially, p.101

8. *Ibid*, p. 102,

9. *Ibid*, p. 102

10. Kapoor, N.D. *Fragrance of Life*, English translation version by Satyandada Arya, Vishwa Jagriti Mission, New Delhi, 1995, p. 51-52

11. Deshpande Nirmala, *More I Have, Less I am in Environmental Ethics*, Gandhi Bhawan, New Delhi 1992 pp. 27-28

12. Mehta, Usha *Education Culture and Mass Communication Discussion on Gandhian Perspective of National Building for World Peace* by N. Radhakrishnan, Konark Publisher Pvt Ltd. New Delhi, 1992. p 126

13. Shukla's *Education in India* Encyclopedia of Social Work in India, Publications Division, New Delhi, 1968 p.264

14. *Ibid*, 265

15. *Ibid*, 265

16. Devikar, *To pupils, with Love*, Miscellany, The Sunday Statesman Review, Sept. 5, 1993, p.5.

17. Young Youth Matiwan, *Lack of Motivation-Primary Case for Decline in Standard View Point* The Nation, Sunday, August 27, 1995, Bangkok (Thailand).

18. Batra, Sunil, *The Thankless Job of Teachers*, The Times of India, Wednesday, September 6,1995, New Delhi, p.12

19. *Ibid* p.12

20. *Ibid* p.20

21. Sharma, S.D., *Illiteracy Reflects on Us, Says Late President on Teacher's Day*, The Times of India, Wednesday, Sept.6, 1995, New Delhi p.5

22. Gangrade K.D., *Building Moral Society through Gandhian Education*, Journal of Higher Education, Vol XVIII No.4 Autumn 1995, pp 553-564.

23. *Gandhi's Autobiography: Moral Lessons*, Gandhi Smriti and Darshan Samiti, New Delhi, 1998, pp XVII and 124.

24. *Ibid*, pp XII and 191

25. Gangrade K.D., *Working with Community at the Grass-root Level: Strategies and Programmes*, Radha Publications, New Delhi, 2001, pp.IX and 444.

26. Kothari L.S., *Education and Peace*, Gandhi Smriti and Darshan Samiti, New Delhi, 2001, pp. 62

27. Swami Chaitanya Keerti, *Universal Love in the Times of Terrorism*, The Hindustan Times, Monday, Sept. 17, 2001, New Delhi p 2.

Education for a Global Society

Baha'i View

Zena Sorabjee

Need for Moral Education

Why is it that at this moment in history we feel an urgent need to look for a new process of moral education? In the past century and a half, humanity has experienced ever more rapid and often revolutionary change. Whether in government or law, in science or industry, or in the relationships between individuals and nations, reevaluation and innovation have become the rule. New knowledge and new understandings are uprooting age-old practices everywhere. Society, in all its aspects, economic, political and cultural, is undergoing a process of fundamental transformation.

Any serious thinking person that searches for the rationale behind world events discovers that there are forces at work and these forces that have to be reckoned with at this historical time are associated with two parallel processes. One process is mostly destructive in nature whilst the other is integrative. The destructive force we see in such phenomena as in the growing racial and religious animosity, spread of terrorism and violence, the breakdown of families, the deterioration of human relations, the increase of suspicion and fear between peoples and nations, the unquenchable thirst for consumerism and misdirected pleasures and the resorting to violence and wrong means to achieve ends. This destructive process is visible and its effects are seen everywhere like September and its aftermath.

It is also seen in the economic disparity in the world where only 20% of the world's population has access to 84% of the wealth of the world. 1.3 billion people earn below $1 per day out of which 350 million are in India. We are subject to 3 levels of inequalities (-) inequality at birth(-) every 3rd child is below 2.3 kg, inequality in later life (-) illiteracy, malnutrition, unemployment and then we have intergenerational inequality with climate change, loss of biodiversity, etc. leaving us handicapped whereas, as Subramania Bharti said the two legs of a human being are nutrition and education.

It is again seen most visibly in the existing moral deficiency in the world. Maurice Strong of the Earth Summit said, "Lack of political will is a moral deficit". Nations and individuals appear to lack the will and capacity to make conscious moral choices. A brilliant scientist does not make a moral choice when he invents a destructive weapon of war which will kill or maim thousands of innocent men, women and children.

We appear to be at a precipice. Destructive forces seem to be pushing the human race towards self-annihilation. Questions are asked, what happened to the values we cherished for thousands of years? How do we remedy our illness? Over 150 years ago *Baha'u'llah*, the Founder of the *Baha'i* Faith gave the solution but the "divine physician" is ignored and we rush to quacks for cures.

Viewing the other process which is constructive in character, does not appear easy. But if we analyse past events in the last 100 years we will recognise that there is a powerful process of integration closely associated and interrelated to the process of disintegration. The most recent example is that of the destructive events of September 11, 2001, forcing a coalition and unity of nations for unified action. This kind of coalition of nations is now being called into being to focus not only on the eradication of terrorism but on the eradication of poverty as well which is one of the causes of terrorism. This suggestion was made by President Gloria Arroyo Macapagal of the Phillippines recently. The integrative process, as it steadily evolves, carries mankind towards an era of fulfillment. Throughout history, the early stages of this process have successively called into being the family unit and its various extensions, the tribe, the city-state and the nation. We now have to develop the clarity of vision to see the distinguishing feature of the present period of history which the integrative process will not yield and which will be its finest fruit: the unification of the entire human race in a world civilisation. This unification, as described in the *Baha'i* writings, will neither "stifle the flame of a sane and intelligent patriotism in men's hearts, nor... abolish the system of national autonomy so essential if the evils of excessive centralisation are to be avoided." It will not attempt to suppress "the diversity of ethnic origins, of climate, of history, of language and tradition, of thought and habit, that differentiate the peoples and nations of the world." It will call for "a wide loyalty," and insist upon "the subordination of national impulses and interests to the imperative claims of a unified world." It will repudiate excessive centralisation on one hand and all attempts at uniformity on the other. Its watchword will be unity in diversity.

Some Concepts of Moral Education

Concepts of moral education are being addressed here today. Old moral codes and belief systems have shown their inadequacy when facing challenges in this age of transformation. We need for humanity to be led out of its confusion and hence there has to be a search for moral codes, ethics and structures with an understanding of the great forces that are operating within every society today. More than a century ago, at the dawn of this period of upheaval and change, *Baha'u'llah* offered insights into the course and direction of history and propounded teachings that would guide humanity through an age of transition to the fulfillment of its long-awaited destiny, its unification.

Modern science and technology have forced us to think in terms of humanity as a whole. And so we would get answers to the many questions if we accepted that collective humanity like an individual goes through the stages of infancy, childhood, adolescence, before maturing into adulthood. Man, having emerged from childhood is now in the stage of turbulent adolescence before entering maturity. That maturity must culminate in the unification of humanity leading to a world civilisation.

A new process of moral education needs to be developed at this time in history. The *Baha'i* writings state, "That which was applicable to human needs during the early history of the race can neither meet nor satisfy the demands of this day, this period of newness and consummation... Man must now become imbued with new virtues and power, new moral standards, new capacities...The gifts and blessings of the period of youth, although timely and sufficient during the adolescence of mankind; are now incapable of meeting the requirement of its maturity" (Modul Baba, 1974).

As we pass through life, we begin to face the fact that our soul in its journey towards God has a great deal to do with *development of spiritual qualities and the acquisition of spirituality*. The son of *Baha'u'llah*, *Abdu'l-Baha*, has given a profound analogy of the child in a mother's womb, developing faculties and physical organs like eyes, ears, teeth, legs, etc. to be used in this world to function with. Similarly, the soul needs to develop spiritual eyes, spiritual understanding—all that we call spiritual qualities including kindness, generosity, honesty, compassion, etc. It is these qualities that our soul carries after death, on its eternal journey. We associate moral education or moral behaviour with those spiritual qualities, with those virtues.

But in this new concept of moral education there is a need to increase the individual's capability of applying those same spiritual principles in making moral choices. The term "capability", as used here, denotes a developed capacity to carry out actions purposefully in a well-defined field of endeavor. In the field of agriculture, for example, the capability to produce a given crop year after year requires that the farmers understand fundamental agricultural concepts, possess skills and abilities that constitute sound agricultural practice, and have a positive attitude towards science and innovation. Similarly, a moral capability results from the interaction of certain related qualities, skills, attitudes and knowledge that enable a person to make moral choices. By focusing attention on the development of moral capabilities on what people must be capable of, not that in order to achieve the two fold purpose of personal and social transformation, it is hoped that the tendency to reduce moral education to sermons on virtues and good behavior will be avoided.

A moral capability indispensable for the construction of a world civilisation is that of building unity. In an age when conflict has become an accepted mode of operation, to be a builder of unity requires far more than a kindly and agreeable personality. It demands, among other things, constant effort to combat prejudice with uncompromising integrity, sensitivity, and compassion. It calls for the ability to identify commonalities, however tenuous, and build on them. It requires the skill of helping people put aside minor disagreements in order to achieve unity within increasingly larger contexts. Other moral capabilities which deserve special attention include those of dealing with others according to the exigencies of unshakable rectitude; of assessing opportunities and selecting means to exploit them with an eye that is free from the self-interest which veils truth; of upholding and defending victims of oppression; of offering solace to the estranged and the suffering; and of bringing joy to the sorrowful and the bereaved.

Some Principles of Moral Education

There are some principles which are unavoidable in the curriculum of moral education. The fundamental one is the all-encompassing principle of the oneness of humankind. This principle is not to stifle the flame of a sane and intelligent patriotism in men's hearts. It will not abolish national autonomy, it will not suppress the diversity of ethnic origins, of language and tradition that differentiate the peoples and nations of the world. But it will call for a wider loyalty and the subordination of national interests to the claims of a unified world. This principle of oneness of mankind is explained in *Baha'i* writings, "...(it) is no mere outburst of ignorant emotionalism or an expression of vague and pious hope. Its appeal is not to be merely identified with a reawakening of the spirit of brotherhood and goodwill among men, nor does it aim solely at the fostering of harmonious cooperation among individual peoples and nations. Its implications are deeper, its claims greater than any which the Prophets of old were allowed to advance. Its message is applicable not only to the essential relationships that must bind all the states and nations as members of one human family. It implies an organic change in the structure of present-day society, a change such as the world has not yet experienced."

The principle of the oneness of mankind enables us to recognise that we are each part of an organic whole and that injury to any part results in injury to all. As the poet John Donne wrote :"No man is an island entire of itself, every man is a part of the whole..." This conviction teaches us that our own fulfillment lies in helping to bring about the welfare and happiness of others.

Understanding Human Nature

Understanding human nature is an essential part of moral education. Man's nature has two aspects, the spiritual and the material. The material side is the product of physical evolution and its end goal is survival. If only this aspect of his nature is concentrated upon, it will have him behave unjustly, cruelly and selfishly. His spiritual nature on the other hand is characterised by love, kindness, generosity and justice. The true station of man is attained when the spiritual side dominates his spirituality existence. Man is in the highest degree of materialism and at the beginning of spirituality that is to say, he is at the end of imperfection and the beginning of perfection. He is at the "last degree of darkness" and at the beginning of light; that is why it has been said that the "condition of man is the end of the night and the beginning of day ..." and that he possesses the degrees of perfection. He has the animal side as well as the angelic side, and the aim of an educator is to so "train human souls that their angelic aspect may overcome their animal side"(Abdul Bahay, 1904).

Attraction to Beauty

A moral person who wants to change the world for the better must allow certain 'forces to shape his sense of purpose. One of those forces is attraction to beauty.

I can have a great deal of purpose but will not be able to achieve it only by my pushing. Forces should pull me and these forces will be forces of attraction and the greater attraction is attraction to beauty. Beauty manifests itself in arts, in music, in crafts, attraction to the beauty of nature, appreciation for the beauty of ideas, for the elegance of scientific theory, for order, for beauty of character. People get pulled towards a beautiful character, as it becomes an attractive force.

Chief among the attributes of good character are trust worthiness and truthfulness. These virtues are the foundation of all the others; without them, neither individual nor social progress is possible. To be trustworthy and truthful, of course, requires far more than to refrain from telling lies. These qualities actually embody the overarching capacity to discern value and uphold truth. When the ability to discern truth is impeded, clarity of thought is unattainable and the capacity to acquire knowledge is also impaired. Indeed, the prosperity of a society depends on the clarity of vision and on the capacity of its people to perceive the truth and act according to its lights. Such perfection and action are the bases of scientific methods and of scientific progress.

Baha'ullah said, "Trustworthiness is the greatest portal leading unto the tranquility and security of the people. In truth the stability of every affair hath depended and doth depend upon it. All the domains of power, of grandeur and of wealth are illumined by its light".

Truthfulness is the foundation of all human virtues. "Without truthfulness, progress and success in all the worlds of God are impossible for any soul. When this holy attribute is established in man, all the divine qualities will also be acquired" (Abdul' Baha, 1990).

Justice

Trustworthiness and truthfulness interact closely with justice, the standard by which individual behavior and the collective actions of society are to be measured. The establishment of world order and the tranquility of the nations depend on justice. Justice is a necessary precondition for the existence of unity and harmony at every level of society. Yet justice cannot be viewed merely as a social necessity. It is a spiritual quality that must adorn every human soul. Through justice and equity, one attains one's own true station. By their light one is able to perceive reality and acquire true knowledge. In order to practice justice one must be able to perceive its implications in interactions with family, friends and community, and clearly recognise the justice or injustice of collective activities in which one participates.

Baha'ullah in Hidden Words said, "The best beloved of all things in My sight is justice; turn not away there from if thou desirest Me and neglect it not that I may confide in thee. By its aid thou shalt see with thine own eyes and not through the eyes of others, and shalt know of thine own knowledge and not through the knowledge of thy neighbor.

Ponder this in thy heart how it behooveth thee to be. Verily justice is My fift to thee and the sign of My loving-kindness. Set it then before thine eyes."

Hence a change which must occur as humanity passes from adolescence to maturity is in its adhering to the principle of justice. Unjust domination of one individual over another, one nation over another, one race over another, one sex over another should be left behind at maturation. Relations of dominance are violent in nature and are many times the result of prejudice. The violence inherent to dominance makes these relations harmful to both the perpetrator and the victim.

Gender Equality

One relation of dominance, which cuts across all lines of class, race or nationality, is that between men and women. Most people do not escape the marks of intimate initiation into this relation of dominance, for exposure to it begins in infancy and continues to affect the growing child throughout its formative years. Within the domestic context the vast majority of humanity learns the habits of dominance, and from this milieu carries them into education, the workplace, political and economic activities, and eventually into all social structures.

The emancipation of women, the achievement of full equality between the sexes, is one of the most important, though less acknowledged prerequisites of peace. The denial of such equality perpetrates an injustice against one-half of the world's population and promotes in men harmful attitudes and habits that are carried from the family to the workplace, to political life, and ultimately to international relations. There are no grounds, moral, practical or biological upon which such denial can be justified. Only if women are welcomed into full partnership in all fields of human endeavor will the moral and psychological climate be created in which international peace can emerge.

Accountability

Training in the principle of accountability is an important aspect of moral education. Law and order can be preserved and upheld if people are convinced that the principle of accountability applies not only in their physical existence but more importantly as their soul journeys towards the Creator and is accountable for its deeds on earth. *Baha'u'llah* urged, "Bring thyself to account each day ere thou art summoned to a reckoning; for death unheralded; shall come upon thee and thou shalt be called to give account for thy deeds."

Man and Nature

There exist at present a predatory relationship between man and his natural environment. A new conception of this relationship must reflect the responsibility to conserve and use rationally the earth's resources and must extend to the very goals and structures according to which society has been organised. Endless acquisition of material goods impelled by individual and collective greed can only aggravate the destruction of the environment. In a world characterised by injustice, the ecological problems created by such behaviour become increasingly unmanageable as hundreds of millions of dispossessed people become victims of, and inadvertently contribute to, the degradation of the environment. The situation becomes further complicated when this system of exploitation, both of nature and of human beings, is carried out in a world ruled by conflict which largely ignores the fact that the bioregions and the interrelationships of nature transcend man-made political boundaries. The process of transforming natural resources into means of well-being of mankind, a proceed that is indispensable for the ongoing advancement of civilisation, must be carried out with the understanding that nature exists in a dynamic balance and that an endless web of relationships exists among all the organisms of the universe:

"Were one to observe with an eye that discovered the realities of all things, it would become clear that the greatest relationship that bindeth the world of being together lieth in the range of created things themselves and that cooperation, mutual aid and reciprocity are essential characteristics in the unified body of the world of being in as much as all created things are closely related together and each is influenced by the other or deriveth benefit therefrom, either directly or indirectly"

As consciousness of the interconnectedness of the universe grows, individuals and groups gain insight into the principle of unity and come to appreciate the beauty and necessity of diversity. If this appreciation for diversity is accompanied by humanity and serenity, progress ceases to be defined by the dictates of arrogance and greed. People then become inclined to choose means and methods for achieving progress that are in harmony with nature.

"Every man of discernment, while walking upon the earth feeleth indeed abashed; in as much as he is fully aware that the thing which is the source of his prosperity, his wealth, his might, his exaltation, his advancement and power is... the very earth which is trodden beneath the feet of all men. There can be no doubt that whoever is cognizant of this truth is cleansed and sanctified from all pride, arrogance, and vainglory" (Bah'au'llah, 1988).

Moral education requires the interaction of the family, school and community.

Final Product

All three components create an atmosphere for the child to be brought up as a purposeful human being whose aim in life is service to his fellow human being. Creating such individuals with this vision of the purpose of their life, a will to render service and a training to perform service, would be the ultimate aim of the new moral education.

References

1. Abdu"l-Baha, cited in Shoghi Effendi, *The World Order of Baha'is: Selected Letters*, Wilmette: Baha'i Publishing Trust, 1974, p.165.
2. 'Abdu'l-Baha, *Some Answered Questions*, Collected and translated from the Persian by Laura Clifford Barney, New Delhi: India Baha'i Publishing Trust, 1996 (reprinted), p 8,9-10
3. Abdu'l-Baha, cited in Shoghi Effendi, *The Advent of Divine Justice*, Wilmette: Baha'i Publishing Trust, 1990, p. 26.
4. *Baha'u'llah, The Hidden Words.*
5. Abdu'l-Baha, cited in *Conservation of the Earth's Resources.*
6. *Baha'u'llah, Epistle to the Son of The Wolf*, Wilmette: Baha'i Publishing Trust, 1988, p 129

Inter-faith Education for an Ever-Advancing Global Society

A.K.Merchant

"Esa devo, visvakarma mahatma sada jananam hrdaye sannivistah,
hrdamanisa mansabhiklpto ya etad viduramrtas te bhavanti"

Svetasvatara Upanishad

More and more young people are becoming disenchanted with an education system that glorifies knowledge built on the shifting sands of relativism. "Where is the wisdom we have lost in knowledge? Where is the knowledge we have lost in information?", a poet asked. The most important feature of *Baha'i* approach to education is its universality. Intellectual and cultural traditions and superstitions are transcended. Herein lie the foundations for the global society. Through education young people can and must be brought to realise their sacred obligation to uphold at all points the cause of universal peace, of world unity, and of cooperative fellowship within one's country and rest of the planet. The learning, then, should transform us into channels of that Divinity endowed with the sense of decency and shame, of duty, of solidarity, of reciprocity and the very feeling of peacefulness, of joy and of hope.

Unfortunately, the individual today has become engulfed in struggles of competitive groups employing different weapons to attain irreconcilable ends. The beginning and end of his actions lie concealed in the fiery smoke of furious, interminable debate and perhaps self-annihilation. His personal world has been transformed into an invaded arena he knows not how to defend. A fresh beginning must be made in our schools and educational institutions and to this end this paper addresses wide ranging issues that urgently concern our country and the world at large. "The turmoil and crisis of our time underlie a momentous transition in human affairs. Simultaneous processes of disintegration and integration have clearly been accelerating throughout the planet for the past century and half, the root causes of which the majority of the world population are only now beginning to fathom. That our earth has contracted into a neighborhood, no one can seriously deny. The world is being made. New Death pangs are yielding to birth pangs. The pain shall wither when members of the human race act upon the common recognition of their oneness. There is a light at the end of this tunnel of change beckoning humanity to the goal destined for it according to the testimonies recorded in all the Holy Books (The Universal House of Justice, 2001). From the human being's inner world of hope and fear, the cry for help has never been raised so desperately nor so universally across the planet. Civilisation is in conflict with the man of nature. Civilisation is betraying the man of understanding and feeling. Why?

Sickness of the soul, like physical ailment, manifests itself in many forms. It need not be a localised pain or an acute sense of shock and disability. An ailment can produce numbness as well as torment, or it can spare the victim's general health but deprive him of sight, hearing or the use of a limb. Soul sickness that goes deep into the core of our being, our psychic organism, seldom finds relief in hysteria or other visible adjustments to ill being. It expresses itself in successive re-orientations to self and to society, each of which results in a conviction representing a definite choice or selection between several possibilities. When the conviction hardens, all possibilities but one are denied and dismissed. If individuals come to realise that effort to express certain qualities through their daily lives is continuously unsuccessful, they will, in the majority of cases, abandon the exercise of that quality and concentrate on others If individuals find that their civilisation makes demands on them for the exercise of qualities they personally condemn, in most cases the necessary adjustment is made.

Where are We Headed?

The individual in present-day society is in the same position as the mountain climber bound himself to other climbers by a rope. At all times, he is compelled to choose between freedom and protection to balance his rights and his loyalties, and compromise between his duty to protect others and his duty to develop something unique and important in himself. As long as the route and the goal are equally vital to all the climbers, the necessary adjustments can be made without undue strain. But modern life binds together, in economic, political, spiritual and other arrangements groups of people who never entered into a pact of mutual agreement, who inwardly desire and need diverse things. The rope that binds them is a tradition, a convention, an inherited obligation to no longer having power to fulfil.

Here, in essence, is the tragic sickness of today's human being. What he sows he cannot reap. What he reaps he cannot store until a new harvest ripens. He feeds on another's desire, he wills to accomplish an alien task, he works to destroy the substance of his dearest hope. Moral standards stop at the frontier of the organised group. Partisan pressures darken the heavens of understanding. Humanity is undergoing a complete transformation of values. The individual is being transplanted from his customary, sheltered traditional way of life to the vast and disruptive confusions of a world in torment. The institutions that have afforded him social or psychic well-being are themselves subject to the same universal dislocation. The label no longer identifies the quality or purpose of the organisation. One cannot retreat into the isolation of primitive simplicity; one cannot advance without becoming a part of a movement of destiny that no one can control nor define.

Where can a new and creative way of life be found? How can people attain knowledge of the means to justify their legitimate hope, fulfil their normal emotions, satisfy their intelligence, unify their aims and civilise their activities? The astronomer has his polished lens of the Hubble Space Telescope and speeding satellites to probe the mysteries of the physical universe. Where can humankind turn to behold the will and purpose of God, the vision of the Cosmic Reality?

What about Conscience?

Many persons feel that in man there is a power of conscience that will unfailingly, like the compass needle, point to the right goal. If in any individual case, the power of conscience fails to operate, it is because the human being himself has betrayed his own divine endowment. He has heard the voice but refused to heed. He has seen the right course of action but preferred to take the evil path. If we examine this contention as applied to ourselves and others familiar to us over a considerable period of time, we find that conscience, as a faculty, cannot be understood by reference to any such naive and conventional view. The individual has no private wire to God. The dictates or impulses we call conscience indicate different course of action at different times. The truth, the law, the appropriate principle or the perfect expression of love is not when conveyed to our minds like a photograph printed from a negative developed in the subconscious self. No individual can afford to rely for guidance in all vital affairs on the testimony offered from within.

Individual conscience appears to be compounded of many ingredients at this stage of mass development: childhood training, personal aptitude, social convention, religious tradition, economic pressure, public opinion and group policy. It is when we examine individual conscience in the area of social action and public responsibility that its limitations become clear. Public policy is the graveyard in which the claim to perfect personal guidance lies interred. In every competitive situation involving social groups, conscientious persons are found on both sides of the struggle. The conscience of one leads to a definition of value or a course of action that stultifies the other. Conscientious persons in the same group seldom agree on matters affecting the whole group. Individual conscience retreats to the realm of the private person when it cannot share or alter the conscience and conviction of others. The result is that while theoretical exaltation of conscience is seldom abandoned, the operation of conscience, outside the small area controlled by personal will, is continuously suppressed. Policy is the conscience of the group, and dominant groups sanction collective actions frequently abhorrent to the individual.

Our dominant groups are the successors to the primitive tribes in which the individual was once completely submerged. Like the primitive tribe, their basic policy is to survive.

So helpless has the individual become under the pressure of world-shaking events that leaders of revolution dismiss their moral worth entirely from their considerations. The individual ceases to be a person. He is made to subject to mass regulation under penalty of punishment for disobedience and, if obedient, under hope of his share of a mass award. Societies have arisen composed of this unmoral mass of human beings, the nature of which resembles the dinosaurs that terrorised the earth millions of years ago.

Between the naive spiritual conception of conscience as divine spark, and the naive rational view that conscience is automatic response to external stimuli, the actual truth undoubtedly lies. Human conscience is a quality existing in different stages of development. In the child it makes for obedience to the power by which the child is protected. It can manifest as an expression of the instinct of self-survival or self development. It can inspire loyalty to the group. It can subject the individual to complete sacrifice for the sake of his group or for the truth he most reveres. Moral attitudes become established through social education and discipline conducted over long periods of time. The moral worth of the individual consists in his capacity to share in a process of endless evolution. Though at times he seems bogged down in the swamp of evil, the ladder of developments stands close to his hand and he can ascend it rung by rung. His moral responsibility can never be disclaimed by him nor voided by others on his behalf, since the principle of cause and effect operates throughout all life. No man and no society exist in a universe shaped in the pattern of human desire.

Conscience is not a form of wisdom or knowledge. It cannot be dissociated from the development of the individual or from the condition of his society. But one may say that conscience is a mirror hung in a room. If the room is darkened, the mirror reflects but dimly. Light is needed—the light of truth, love and justice. Then will the mirror of spiritual awareness disclose to the individual the essential nature of his own problem of choice, and open for him the door that leads from the private person to humankind? The helplessness of the individual today is due to the absence of light. The *Baha'i* writings state, "When man allows the spirit, through his soul, to enlighten his understanding, then does he contain all creation; because man, being the culmination of all that went before and thus superior to all previous evolutions, contains all the lower world within himself illuminated by the spirit through the instrumentality of the soul, man's radiant intelligence makes him the crowning-point of creation. But on the other hand, when man does not open his mind and heart to the blessing of the spirit, but turns his soul towards the material side, towards the bodily part of his nature, then is he fallen from his high place and he becomes inferior to the inhabitants of the lower animal kingdom. In this case, the man is in a sorry plight. For if the spiritual qualities of the soul, open to the breath of the Divine Spirit, are never used, they become atrophied, enfeebled, and at last incapacitated; while the soul's material qualities alone being exercised, they become terribly powerful and the unhappy, misguided man becomes more savage, more unjust, more vile, more cruel, more malevolent than the lower animals themselves. If, on the contrary, the spiritual nature of the soul has been so strengthened that it holds the material side in subjection, then does the man approach the divine; his humanity becomes so glorified that the virtues of the celestial assembly are manifest in him; he radiates the mercy of God, he stimulates the spiritual progress of mankind, for he becomes a lamp to show light on their path (Abdul Baha, 1971).

Thus two paths that open before each human being, the choice of which he himself is free to make, namely continuing to perpetrate unimaginable horrors and sufferings through stubborn clinging to old patterns of behaviour, or to establish by an act of united endeavour lasting peace, harmony and a reign of righteousness. If individual conscience cannot illumine from man's inner world the nature of basic social problems, what of religion? Have the traditional faiths such command of spiritual truth that they can serve as the guide and conscience of human kind? Do these sects and denominations constitute the moral compass bestowing vision upon a divided, a desperate humanity? Has our Creator communicated to our age from these minarets, these temples, mosques, chapels and churches that represent the meaning and purpose of true religion to the masses in the East and the West?

The world of sectarian religion is not a universe, ordered by one central creative will, but the fragments of a world which no human authority has power to restore. The major religions known in our country—Hinduism, Buddhism, Jainism, Zoroastrianism, Judaism, Christianity, Islam and Sikhism are standing apart like continents separated by unchartered seas despite the regular inter-faith exchanges and the mushrooming of inter-religious organisations. There are in each of these bodies a large number of independent, mutually exclusive subdivisions. Their diverse claims to organic sovereignty maintain in the realm of faith the same condition that exists among the nation-states. They deal with one another according to bilateral and multilateral treaties and international agreements, protocols and conventions, all without control of the greater and vital movements of society or even foreknowledge of what was and is to come.

This is why humanity has suffered two world wars, social dislocation and a plague of immorality, faithlessness, materialism and discontent. No universal religious body has existed to stay the swift descent of our age into the gloom of savage strife. Events do not wait upon doctrinal readjustments. When peace does not exist in the world of the soul, it cannot exist in any other realm of human intercourse and experience. The masses have been given no moral unity, no common purpose which, stamped with divine authority, could raise them above the fatal disunities and conflicts distilled by their economic and political institutions. Yet each of these Faiths was divinely revealed, imbued with a universal spirit, charged with a high creative mission, and established itself through the sacrifice and heroism of those early followers who beheld the Cosmic Force. Each Faith has reconsecrated human life and by its lifeblood nourished great progress in civilisation. What has happened to the first, true vision? What has extinguished the flame upon the altar of worship?

The super human character of revelation has gradually undergone dilution and admixture. The human explanation of a truth has been substituted for the truth itself. The performance of ceremonial rites has come to occupy the place held by the mystery of spiritual rebirth. Obligation to a professionalised institution has weakened the duty laid upon individuals to serve society and humankind. The aim of a regenerated, righteous, peaceful civilisation inspired by the founders of religion has become diverted into hope for the victory of the church or the *guru*. Sectarianism in essence is not freedom of religion.

All things exist in a process of life and death, growth and development, extinction and renewal. The fact that what men devise as a counterfeit for truth is eventually destroyed, does not confirm the rejection of religion by the cynic or the materialist. On the contrary, the succession of Faiths throughout the period of known history points to a complete vindication of the Faith in God, since He divides truth from error, the spirit from the letter. He punishes and He rewards. For every death, He sends a new life, "O army of life!" The *Baha'i* teachings warn, "East and West have joined to worship stars of faded splendour and have turned in prayer unto darkened horizons. Both have utterly neglected the broad foundation of God's sacred laws, and have grown unmindful of the merits and virtues of His religion. They have regarded certain customs and conventions as the immutable basis of the Divine Faith, and have firmly established themselves therein.

They have imagined themselves as having attained the glorious pinnacle of achievement and prosperity when, in reality, they have touched the innermost depths of heedlessness and deprived themselves wholly of God's bountiful gifts. The corner stone of the Religion of God is the acquisition of the Divine perfection and the sharing in His manifold bestowals. The essential purpose of faith and belief is to ennoble the inner being of man with the outpourings of grace from high. If this be not attained, it is indeed deprivation itself. It is the torment of infernal fire" (*Abdul Baha* 1942).

And even more definitely, "Superstitions have obscured the fundamental reality, the world is darkened and the light of religion is not apparent. This darkness is conducive to differences and dissensions; rites and dogmas are many and various; therefore, discord has arisen among the religious systems, whereas religion is for the unification of mankind. True religion is the source of love and agreement amongst men/women, the cause of development of praiseworthy qualities; but the people are holding to the counterfeit and imitation, negligent of the reality which unifies, so they are bereft and deprived of the radiance of religion" (Abdul Baha, 1976). "When the lights of religion become darkened and materialists appear they are the bats of night; the decline of religion is their time of activity; they seek the shadows when the world is darkened and the clouds have spread over it" (Abdul Baha, 1976). If the edifice of religion shakes and totters, commotion and chaos will ensue and the order of things will be utterly upset (Abdul Baha, 1976). "Religious fanaticism and hatred," *Baha'u'llah* affirms, "are a world-devouring fire, whose violence none can quench. The Hand of Divine Power can alone deliver mankind from this desolating affliction" (*Baha'u'llah*, 1973).

Religious Fanaticism and Nationalism in the Era of Globalisation

When changes take place in the spiritual life of a people, they produce effects not only upon the realm of personal conscience or upon the definitions of denominational faith. Their results flow forth throughout the civilisation. Society, indeed, is the outer surface of human action, as religion is the inner surface. The persons who are impressed with certain values from the religious teaching of their childhood, strive to fulfill them as adults in their civilisation. The nations of the world are not composed of a separate race of human beings called citizens or subjects; all this mass of humanity who serve as citizens or subjects are at the same time members of different ethnic groups and members of different religious bodies. Since religious training has for the most part been based upon pre-rational states of childhood, the vital assumptions of Faith or theology continue from generation to generation without analysis or investigation. The child assumes that his religion sets him off, in some mysterious but inevitable and justifiable mailer, from those people who belong to a different religion. This pre-rational experience becomes an imperative directing his activities in other fields, all the more effective because it works behind his conscious and rational thought. Religion has thus prepared the way for the spirit of exclusive nationalism, class competition and other self-centered types of social institution. The pre-rational experience of justifiable division matures in the irrational attitudes of partisan loyalty that set people off from one another in political and economic matters, eventuating in strife and ruin.

The modern nation represents the most powerful and effective social unity ever achieved. It has coordinated the human qualities and possibilities to an unprecedented degree, liberating people from servitude to nature and laying the foundations of orderly progress by reconciling the political claims of the state with the social and cultural needs of the individual. But like every human institution, the nation cannot become an end unto itself. It cannot draw arbitrary lines and decree that human evolution must stop short at this line or that. The nation cannot reduce all questions of human relations to political principle, and solve them by a formal relationship to the state.

The movement of life is irresistible. When the modern nation had organised its area and completed the creation of the necessary institutions, it became mature and incurred obligation to establish useful relationships with other nations. The nation became more and more involved in activities and affairs outside its boundaries and beyond its jurisdiction. The process of globalisation that had its genesis in internationalism has been the principle of civilisation for over a century, but the nations cannot realise themselves as means to an end, as instruments called upon, for the sake of humanity, to create sovereignty of and for the entire world. This moral resolution has been lacking.

Denied fulfillment in world order, present-day globalisation has organised the nations for their own destruction. The social organism made an end unto itself becomes self consuming. First, there has been an interval of spiritual blindness, a miscalculation of the essential nature of the human being; then a denial of the obligation to join with other nations for the sake of peace; a denunciation of some threatening foe, and, finally, a plunge into the maelstrom where every trend towards world unity is accelerated faster than the public intelligence can comprehend.

Power to make permanent and workable decisions has been temporarily lost. Our international relations rest upon formal bilateral and multi-lateral agreements, treaties, protocols and conventions that are now increasingly impacting world relationships. However, this is far from satisfactory because experience shows that often these binding documents are set aside if the strains of social dislocation go to the breaking point. In such a condition of crisis, humanity finds itself unable to return to the simpler societies of the past and unable to generate sufficient power for true unity in a world civilisation. Thus, globalisation with all of its positive intentions is often reduced to succumbing to the push and pulls of the market forces, to the whims and fancies of multi-national and trans-national corporations, to the foreign policies of a few big powers. The races and peoples, as repeatedly demonstrated by the series of United Nations Conferences and Conventions, meet in a fateful encounter, each cherishing its separateness as a duty and a right. One may say that humanity does not yet exist, for men are not directed by a world consciousness or impelled by a mutual faith.

"Today the world of humanity," the *Baha'i* writings stated nearly a century ago, "is in need of international unity and conciliation. To establish these great fundamental principles, a propelling power is needed. It is self-evident that unity of the human world and the Most Great Peace cannot be accomplished through material means. They cannot be established through political power, for the political interests of nations are various and the policies of peoples are divergent and conflicting. They cannot be founded through racial or patriotic power, for these are human powers, selfish and weak. The very nature of racial differences and patriotic prejudices prevents the realisation of this unity and agreement. Therefore, it is evidenced that the promotion of the oneness of the kingdom of humanity, which is the essence of the teachings of all the Manifestations of God, is impossible except through the divine power and the breaths of the Holy Spirit. Other powers are too weak and are incapable of accomplishing this" (Abdul Baha, 1942).

It is therefore, through this Cosmic Power, the human beings should free themselves from the captivity of the world of his lower nature; for as long as he is captive of the physical world, the humans will struggle like the animals since the struggle for existence is one of the exigencies of the material world. This urge of struggle for existence is the basic source of all calamities and a supreme affliction in present-day society.

Spiritual Education and Peaceful Living

In the *Baha'i* writings, peace is revered because in essence it is a spiritual mystery in which humanity has been invited in our day, for the first time, to partake. Peace is a divine creation, a reconciliation of human and divine purpose. Thus, the issues of human existence turn upon the axis of education. Education alone can overcome the inertia of our separateness, transmute our creative energies for the realisation of world unity, free the mind from its servitude to the past and reshape civilisation to be the guardian of our spiritual and physical resources.

The teachings of *Baha'u'llah*, upon which the *Baha'i* philosophy of education is based, describe each human being as "a mine rich in gems of inestimable value" (*Baha'u'llah*, 1973). He is neither a fallen creature nor merely the product of socio-economic forces; the individual is a phenomenon of limitless potentialities intellectual, emotive, moral, and spiritual.

The true purposes of education are not fulfilled by the knowledge conferred through civil education, since this knowledge ends with the purposes of the individual or the needs of the state. They are not fulfilled by sectarian education, since sectarian knowledge excludes the basic principle of the continuity and progressiveness of revelation. The true purposes of education are not achieved by independent pursuit of knowledge undertaken through study of the classics, and the great philosophies or even the religious systems of the past. Such education enhances the individual capacity and deepens the insight of a group. It opens the door to a world of superior minds and heroic accomplishment. But that world is the reflection of the light of truth upon past conditions and events. It is not the rising of the sun to illumine our own time, inspire a unified world movement, and regenerate withered souls. Nor may we hope that psychology can develop the necessary transforming power for a dislocated society, a scientific substitute for the primitive offices of religion. The explorer in the world of the psyche sees the projection of his own shadow, finds the answer determined by his own question. He/she can prove mechanistic determinism or demonstrate the freedom and responsibility of the soul. The area within which he works is suitable for the development of personal healing. He can learn the habitual reactions of persons in a group or of groups in a society, but this knowledge is statistical until applied by a comprehensive organ of intelligence on a world scale.

"The human spirit which distinguishes man from the animal," the *Baha'i* teachings state, "is the rational soul; and these two names—the human spirit and the rational soul designate one thing. This spirit, which in the terminology of the philosophers is the rational soul, embraces all beings, and as far as human ability permits, discovers the realities of things and becomes cognizant of their peculiarities and effects, and of the qualities and properties of beings. But the human spirit, unless assisted by the spirit of faith, does not become acquainted with the divine secrets and the heavenly realities. It is like a mirror which, although clear, polished and brilliant, is still in need of light. Until a ray of the sun reflects upon it, it cannot discover the heavenly secrets" (Abdul Baha, 1976). Elsewhere, *Baha'i* writings affirm, "With the love of God, all sciences are accepted and beloved, but without it, are fruitless; nay, rather, the cause of insanity. Every science is like unto a tree, if the fruit of it is the love of God, that is a blessed tree. Otherwise it is dried wood and finally a food for fire" (Abdul Baha, 1976). A new and universal concept of education is found in the writings of the *Baha'i* Faith and for the sake of brevity we are able to share only a few extracts.

"When we consider existence, we see that the mineral, vegetable, animal and human worlds are all in need of an educator".

"If the earth is not cultivated, it becomes a jungle where useless weeds grow; but if a cultivator comes and tills the ground, it produces crops which nourish living creatures. It is evident, therefore, that the soil needs the cultivation of the farmer".

"The same is true with respect to animals: notice that when the animal is trained, it becomes domestic, and also, that man, if he is left without training becomes bestial, and, moreover, if left under the rule of nature, he becomes lower than an animal, whereas if he is educated he becomes an angel."

"Now reflect that it is education that brings the East and the West under the authority of man; it is education that produces wonderful industries; it is education that spreads glorious sciences and arts; it is education that makes manifest new discoveries and laws. If there were no educators there would be no such things as comforts, civilisation, facilities, or humanity."

"But education is of three kinds: material, human and spiritual. Material education is concerned with the progress and development of the body, through gaining its sustenance, its material comfort and ease. This education is common to animals and man."

"Human education signifies civilisation and progress, that is to say, government, administration, charitable works, trades, arts and handicrafts, sciences, great inventions and discoveries of physical laws, are the activities essential to man as distinguished from the animal."

"Divine education is that of the Kingdom of God: it consists in acquiring divine perfections, and this is true education; for in this estate, man becomes the centre of divine appearance, the manifestation of the words, 'Let us make man in our image and after our likeness'. This is the supreme goal of the world of humanity."

"Now we need an educator who will be at the same time a material, human and spiritual educator, and whose authority will be effective in all conditions."

"It is clear that human power is not able to fill such a great office, and that the reason alone could not undertake the responsibility of so great a mission. How can one solitary person without help and without support lay the foundations of such a noble construction? He must depend on the help of the spiritual and divine power to be able to undertake this mission. One Holy Soul gives life to the world of humanity, changes the aspect of the terrestrial globe, causes intelligence to progress, vivifies souls, lays the foundation of a new existence, establishes the basis of a marvelous creation, organizes the world, brings nations and religions under the shadow of one standard, delivers man from the world of imperfections and vices, and inspires him with the desire and need of natural and acquired perfections. Certainly nothing short of a divine power could accomplish so great a work" (Abdul Baha, 1996).

For these reasons, the re-education—the transformation—of the human beings of today is contingent upon the emergence of a culture in which universal spiritual values are dominant. In essence, this is the basic rationale underlying the *Baha'i* perspective on education. In a statement issued during the International Year of Literacy in 1988, the *Baha'i* International Community proposed the following as compelling goals in providing an education for the wholesome development of young people at all levels of the society:

1. The realisation that it is chiefly service to humanity and dedication to the unification of mankind that unlock individual capacity and release creative powers latent in human nature.

2. The understanding that the mere knowledge of principles is insufficient to ensure personal growth and social change, that both require the exercise of volition and application of will.

3. A firm conviction that human honour and happiness lie in self-respect and noble purposes, in integrity and moral equality, and not in the mere pursuit of wealth and power for their own sake.

4. A reasonable degree of excellence in at least one productive skill through which individuals can experience the truth that work is

worship when performed in a spirit of service, and can secure the means of existence with dignity and honour.

5. An adequate understanding of some of the concerns of programmes of social progress, such as health and sanitation, agriculture, crafts and industry, environment and ecology, at least in the local or regional context.

6. Some development of the individual's capacity for intellectual investigation as a distinguishing power of the human mind and as an indispensable instrument for successful community action.

7. Some capacity to analyse social conditions and discover the forces that have caused them, and corresponding ability to express ideas, so as to be able to contribute to consultation on community problems.

8. The capacity to take part in community planning and action as a determined yet humble participant who helps overcome conflict and division and contributes to the establishment of a spirit of unity and collaboration.

9. A disposition to analyse and desire to understand the features of different forms of government, law and public administration.

These precepts are not advanced in abstract, but are based on real experience. Although the *Baha'i* community cannot claim to have created its desired system of universal education, it feels encouraged by the progress of its several decades of organised educational efforts. Moreover, it is convinced that principles underlying its approach are applicable universally and can contribute to a global campaign to extend the benefits of education to the generality of humankind. The application of these principles does not necessarily imply a prolonged educational programme, where circumstances do not immediately make this practicable. For children, the process is set in motion in early childhood as a concerned effort to develop character and encourage the emergence of spiritual qualities latent in human nature (Abdu'l Baha, 1976).

The Role of Inter-faith Values in Education

The focal point of the *Baha'i* education is a clarification of man's relationship with the divine Creator; as long as peoples differ or are unaware, or accept a substitute for this relationship, we cannot distinguish between truth and error, or discriminate between principle and superstition. Until we apprehend human beings in the light of the creative purpose, it is impossible to know others or ourselves. Social truth is merely experiment and hypothesis unless it forms part of a spiritual reality. The founders of revealed religions or *Dharma*, who have been termed prophets, messengers, *avataras*, messiahs, the *tirthankaras* and the *tathagathas*, in the *Baha'i* teachings are designated Manifestations of God. These beings, walking on earth as men, stand in a higher order of creation and are endowed with powers and attributes that transcend human limitations. In the world of truth they shine like the sun, and the rays emanating from that sun are the light and the life of the souls of men.

The Manifestation is not God. The Infinite cannot be incarnated. God reveals His will through the Manifestation, and apart from what is thus manifested His will and reality remain forever unknown. The physical universe does not reveal the divine purpose for human civilisation. "The holy Manifestations of God, the divine prophets, are the first teachers of the human race. They are universal educators and the fundamental principles they have laid down are the causes and factors of the advancement of nations. Forms and imitations which creep in afterward are not conducive to that progress. On the contrary these are destroyers of the human foundations laid by the heavenly educators (Abdu'l Baha, 1976). "Every one of them," the *Baha'i* teachings state, "is the Way of God that connects this world with the realms above, and the standard of His truth unto every one in the kingdoms of earth and heaven. They are the Manifestations of God amidst men, the evidences of His truth, and the signs of His glory" (Abdu' Baha, 1976). They are the channels of the Cosmic Force and "in whom the spiritual and moral urges and loyalties of the age were focused. They are the embodiment of its spiritual dynamics. Such a Saviour, or the Avatara, unlike ordinary saints and seers, is not a static lighthouse." He, in the words of Shri Ramakrishna, "is a large-sised ship capable of carrying thousands of people across the water of life. He appears on the world scene to establish *Dharma* (justice and righteousness) in the words of Shri Krishna; and He sets in motion the wheel of

Dharma, says the Lord Buddha in the first sermon. The *Avatara* as understood in India is an epoch-maker, a spiritual dynamo from which man-making and nation-making forces emanate to accelerate the process of the spiritual evolution of humanity. He is a world transformer and in Him an idea becomes yoked to will, purpose and endeavour. He is the dominating spiritual hero of an epoch which functions as a dynamic source of a creative social process, and the sustenance and guide of an egalitarian social order" (Ranganathananda, 1960).

The whole pattern and process of history rests upon the succession of dispensations by which man's innate capacities are developed and by which the course of social evolution is sustained. The rise and fall of civilisations proceed as the effect of prior spiritual causation. An ancient civilisation undergoes moral decadence; by division of its own people and attack from without, its power and authority are destroyed; and with that destruction collapses the culture and the religious system which had become parasites upon its material wealth. Concurrently, a new creative spirit reveals itself in the rise of a greater and better type of society from the ruins of the old.

The critical point in this process is the heroic sacrifice offered to the prophet or the *avatara* by those who see in Him the way to God, and His official condemnation by the heads of the prevailing systems of *dharma* or religion. That condemnation, because men cannot judge God, recoils back upon the religion and civilisation itself. They have condemned themselves. Whilst the small number of those who have recognised the new Manifestation of God grow from strength to strength. The future is with them. In their spiritual fellowship the seeds of the new civilisation are watered and its first, tender growth safeguarded by their heart's blood.

Through the Manifestation of God, the power of the Holy Spirit accomplishes the will of God. Nothing can withstand that power. Because its work is not instantaneous, a darkened age cannot perceive the awful process of cause and effect—the divine will as cause, and human history as effect—guiding human destiny from age to age. However, the *Baha'i* writings penetrate farther into the mystery of divine manifestations when they affirm that in spirit and in aim the successive messengers are one being, one authority, one will. This teaching of the oneness of the Manifestations of God is the essential characteristic of a revelation that represents religion of *dharma* for the cycle of humankind's maturity and the establishment or peace.

"There can be no doubt whatever," *Baha'u'llah* says, "that the people of the world, of whatever race or religion, derive their inspiration from one heavenly source and are the subjects of one God. The difference between the ordinances under which they abide should be attributed to the varying requirements of the age in which they were revealed" (*Baha'ir Kala* 1973). Those who deny and condemn the *avatara* or the prophet, therefore, are not defending the divine purpose from sinister betrayal by one who introduces new laws and principles; on the contrary, since the Manifestation in Himself is one, they condemn their own saviour when He returns to regenerate the world and advance the true Faith of God. Thus is the moral nature of human life, and man's responsibility to God, sustained throughout the devious course of history. Faith is no mere belief; but a connection with the only power that confers immortality on the soul and saves humanity as a whole from complete self-destruction.

"A man who has not had a spiritual education," *Baha'i* writings attest, "is a brute" (Abdu'l Baha, 1996). "We have decreed, a people, that the highest and last end of all learning be the recognition of Him who is the Object of all knowledge; and yet behold how you have allowed your learning to shut you out, as by a veil, from Him who is the Day-spring of this Light, through whom every hidden thing has been revealed" (*Baha'ullah*, 1988). The oneness of the divine intermediaries has been thus established in the *Baha'i* writings, "In the World of God there is unity, the oneness of the Manifestations of God. There is unity divine, heavenly, radiant, merciful; and the one reality appearing in successive manifestations. For instance, the sun is one and the same but its points of dawning are various. During the summer season it rises from the northern point of the ecliptic; in winter it appears from the southern point of rising. Although these dawning-points are different, the sun is the same sun which has appeared from them all. The significance is the reality of prophethood which is symbolised by the sun, and the holy Manifestations are the dawning-places or zodiacal points" (Abdu'l Baha, 1976).

This knowledge offers our society the substance of the education needed for the establishment of a society worthy of the blessings of justice and peace. At the very least, the pressure of historical circumstances and the crisis in every aspect of present-day life besetting our nation in particular and humanity in general should persuade the inhabitants of this land to have a closer and impartial look at the *Baha'i* philosophy and practice of education, to estimate its indispensability in the light of contemporary problems, even if they have, through ignorance, apathy or complacency, ignored it at first. For to the degree that the peoples and nations of the world accept the Teachings of *Baha'u'llah* and work through the principles, channels and institutions provided by Him for the unification of humankind, to that degree will they be able to transform their own inner lives, reconstruct their societies, and contribute substantially to the advent of that universal and divine family of man—*Vasudhaiva Kutumbakam* which is the ideal and fulfillment of both the *dharma* and religion, whatever may be our beliefs and methods of interpretation (Raman, 1986).

Conclusion

At the heart of the *Baha'i* philosophy of education is a spiritual conception of the nature of the individual and society. What has been described in the foregoing are some of the central principles guiding the *Baha'i* community in its initial attempt to follow the path of development traced for it in the writings of its Founders. The creation of a coherent system of universal education that adequately embodies this vision is a task that lies in the future. Experimental beginnings can be seen in the wide diversity of *Baha'i* schools to be found around the world. These range from simple tutorial centres at the village level to schools that offer classes from the pre-school level to tertiary levels. The schools are open to all the students and not only to *Baha'i* families. Budding programmes in adult literacy carried out by *Baha'i* Councils and Assemblies throughout the world augments the work of the schools. At the international level, the *Baha'i* community has undertaken a major coordinated plan that supports the decade's long effort to eliminate illiteracy and promote "education for all" that was launched by the United Nations.

The optimism that *Baha'is* feel about humanity's capacity to meet the global educational challenge arises not only from their own experience but also from a firm belief that "whatever suffering and turmoil the years immediately ahead may hold, however dark the immediate circumstances be, human can confront this supreme trial with confidence in its ultimate outcome. Far from signalizing the end of civilisation, the convulsive changes towards which humanity is being ever more rapidly impelled will serve to release the 'potentialities inherent in the station of man' and reveal the full measure of his destiny on earth, the innate excellence of his reality" (The Universal House of Justice, 1985). Most of the necessary expertise already exists in a wide range of governmental, academic and other agencies. Around the world, examples abound of the capacity of people to create grass roots networks to tackle such urgent local problems as deficient educational systems. What is needed to ensure success in this global endeavor is unity. "So powerful is the light of unity", *Baha'u'llah* affirmed over a hundred years ago, "that it can illuminate the whole earth" (*Baha'u'llah*, 1973).

References

1. The Universal House of Justice, Baha'i World Centre, Haifa, letter dated 22 May 2001 written on the occasion of the official opening of the Terraces of the Shrine of the Bab (Prophet-Herald of the *Bahai Faith*), 22 May 2001.
2. 'Abdu'l-Baha. *The Reality of Man—Excerpts from the Writings of Baha'ullah and Abdu'l-Baha*, New Delhi, India, Baha'i Publishing Trust, 1971, pp 12-13.
3. 'Abdu'l-Baha, *Selected Writings of 'Abdu'l-Baha*, Wilmette, USA: Baha'i Publishing Trust, 1942, pp 43-44.
4. '*Abdu'l-Baha, Some Answered Questions*, Collected and translated from the Persian by Laura Clifford Barney, New Delhi: India Baha'i Publishing Trust, 1996 (reprinted), p 8-10.

5. *Baha'u'llah, Epistle to the Son of The Wolf*, Wilmette: Baha'i Publishing Trust, 1988, p 129.

6. Baha'u'llah, *Gleaning from the Writings of Baha'u'llah*, New Delhi, India Baha'i Publishing Trust, 1973, Section CXXXII p 288.

7. Raman, S.P., *My Quest in the Fulfillment of Hinduism*, New Delhi: India Baha'i Publishing Trust. 1986, p 17.

8. Ranganathananda, Swami, *Eternal Values for a Changing Society*, Calcutta: Advaita Ashram, 1960, p 34.

A Scientific Vision of Education
for a Global Society

Sampooran Singh

The twentieth century has been dominated by science and technology. Our present education is geared to industrialisation and war. Its principal aim is to develop efficiency and we are caught in this machine of ruthless competition and mutual destruction. It leads to war, and it teaches us to destroy or be destroyed. It leads us to secondary values, merely making us proficient in some branch of knowledge and ignoring the wholeness of life.

Modern science has shown that all its theories of natural phenomena, including the 'laws' they describe are creations of the human mind; properties of our conceptual map of reality rather than of reality itself, or parts of the map, not of the territory. Every activity of mind leads to enhancing matter content called conditioning of the psyche, which results in lowering the sensitivity of mind and increase of entropy (self-annihilation or death). A mind that has been merely trained in continuation of the past does not have the capacity to discover and thus becomes a mechanical golem, a repetitive process. It rejects intuition. It cannot integrate the right hemisphere and the left hemisphere of the brain, even action leads to fragmentation, and life becomes a series of conflicts and sorrows.

What we call education is a matter of accumulating (or storing as memory) information and knowledge from books. Conflict and confusion result from our own wrong relationship with people, things and ideas, leading to chaos and destruction. It appears that education has utterly failed.

Contemporary Concerns

Frederico Mayor Zaragoza, Director-General of UNESCO, in a conference where seventy-four leading scientists (including Nobel Laureates) and eminent politicians had gathered, stated:

> "Never before, until now, has the tension between science and the human conscience, between technology and ethics, reached a point where it has become a threat to the world as a whole. We are so dazzled that we do not perceive the threats hanging over our heads, warning us of the pressing need for a radically new and universally ethical outlook on the future of present-day science."

Bertrand Russell wrote, "Whatever else may be mechanical, values are not, and this is something which no political philosopher must forget". He added, "Unless men increase in wisdom as much as in knowledge, increase of knowledge will be increase of sorrow". Values arise from the depth dimension (subjective) of man. A Nobel Prize winning Biologist, Jacques Monod, gave a final appraisal of our situation:

> "The choice of scientific practice has launched the evolution of culture on a one way path: onto a track which nineteenth-century scientism saw leading infallibly upward an empyrean noon hour for mankind, whereas what we see opening before us today is an abyss of darkness."

George Wald, Nobel Laurreatte in Medicine, 1967, wrote:

> "Our society has taken a wrong turn. In our thirst for knowledge, we have cut ourselves off from wisdom. In our pride in science, we have come to despise and reject intuitive and instinctual perceptions that have heretofore animated and given perspective and hope and meaning of human existence. By now the problem is not transcendence, but survival. If we are to survive there must be fundamental changes in direction too, not only organisation, but in our ways of thinking. We have to think different thoughts and to want different things."

The basic cause of the failure of education is that man engaged himself in the sensual world, the external world of time-space matrices. The objective world neglected the inner world, the subjective dimension of man. The conditioned mind has constructed the time-space matrices in quick succession and this has led to a crisis of perception, or psychic pandemic, a psychic contagious epidemic. The crisis of perception is defined as unawareness of the *truth*, the present, the fact and awareness of the false, the past, the non-fact, the what should be. It is grafting of ideals or concepts on pure perception, or in the language of physics, it is incoherent super positions of the past on the present. It is an unprecedented crisis which has global dimensions.

The reports submitted by the Brandt Commission (1977), the Palme Commission (1980), and the Brundtland Commission (1987) were firmly based on the concept of common responsibility for the future of our planet and also attached importance to the concept of interdependence, though with varying emphasis. The notions of "common interests", "common security", and "common future" demand that uncompromising confrontations should be ended throughout the World and give way to harmonious coexistence.

According to the findings of the World Commission on Environment and Development (WCED) and of the United Nations Environment Programme (UNEP), humanity is now able to bring about radical changes on the planet Earth, which may either take a destructive or constructive course. The United Nations Conference on Disarmament and Development held in 1987 also came to the conclusion that disarmament, development and security are interdependent. In spite of all these efforts at the highest echelons, many environmentalists are of the opinion that ecological challenges for instance, global warming are increasing at an accelerative pace.

The UNESCO Commission presided over by M. Edgar Faure, in 1972 published a book *Learning to Be: The World of Education Today and Tomorrow*. The book emphasizes that the "physical, intellectual, emotional, and ethical integration of the individual into a complete man is a broad definition of the fundamental aim for education."

The UNESCO International Commission, chaired by Jacques Delor, Report (1996), titled *Learning: The Treasure Within* identified four pillars of education, which are:

(i) Learning to Know

(ii) Learning to Do

(iii) Learning to Be

(iv) Learning to Live Together. It is a declaration of paradigm shift from without to within, from objective to subjective, from science to spirituality.

In a scientific conference, Russian scientists have come up with the idea of a Life Field beyond our own physical concepts of time, space and the known electro-magnetic and gravitational fields. Another conference at Cambridge proposed that a new scientific approach would include subjective experience as valid information and address all forms of human experience including intuition, spirituality and mystical encounters.

That the "man is infinite", there is "Life Field" and the "cosmos is interconnected" are almost knocking at the cathedral of ancient Indian discoveries in the Vedas and Upanishads. Scientists have recovered something mysteriously rich in energy (at very high frequency, higher frequency means higher energy), in empty space (the void). Now we are on the verge of extending this richness into human dimensions. This is perhaps the only vocation of mankind.

Modern science concludes that we have to learn to live in a higher awareness to resolve the challenge. This is precisely what the ancient India cultural heritage advocates. Modern science advocates that life is infinite and is governed by Universal Consciousness. The *Vedic* Wisdom also concludes that all life emerges from Brahman, the Universal Consciousness.

The foundation of education for a global society is to perceive this rich energy, the Life Field, and then live in the light of that communion with the laws of nature. This paper presents a renewed look at the meaning and significance of the wholeness of life. It investigates psycho-names (self-knowledge) of conditioned psyche (apparent world, objective world); and exploration of unconditioned energy (intrinsic world, the subjective world, the substratum of existence, and the void). The investigation of conditioned psyche flows into understanding and learning, intuition (insight) and spontaneity. The exploration of intrinsic world, or the subjective nature of man leads to vibration Life Field (Active Reality) and vibrationless Life Field (Passive Reality). The insight or communion with nature is holy and sacred, and therefore we call it the journey to the Sacred Temple of Understanding and Learning, which is the right kind of global education.

Individual and Society

Man has created a culture, which has resulted into society. The action of relationship between different human beings is society; and that society is invariably static. Society is static while man is dynamic. We have constructed a society which is "repetitive, disintegrating and static." Society is the product of relationship and if our relationship is confused, egocentric, limited, we project that relationship which expresses itself as chaos, disorder and disharmony into the world. Society has no life-giving quality. Thus any action, any reform, any legislation in the external field, which deals with distorted man-made social cosmos, becomes equally static. Mere transformation of the outer is meaningless and has no significance. The intellectual values have no capacity to bring in radical transformation in the conditioned psyche. What you are, the world is. So our problem is the world's problem. Society exists for convenience of man for communication, action and living; and not that man exists for sustaining the society or to fit into a known social order (Krishnamoorthy: 1977).

Man has erred in having his values as accumulation of money, bank balance and property; acquiring car, television set, refrigerator, air conditioner, and so on, which lead to position, prestige and power in the man-made society. This is what man wants but society wants them to fit into the pattern of values.

The problem is never static. It is always present, whether it is a problem of hunger, starvation and poverty, or violence or fear, or any other psychological imbalance. Any crisis is always new, therefore it must be understood in its wholeness. It can only be understood by non-symbolic, non-dualistic, non-conceptual frame of reference of mind spectrum, which is always fresh and clear, and it can follow the problem swiftly in its pursuit. We urgently need a radical transformation of the dualistic frame to non-dual frame, because it can bring about a transformation in the outer society. We have to deeply understand the psycho-dynamics of the conditioned mind-brain-body system, because the inner and the outer are a single dynamic movement—one whole. The transformation in the society cannot happen without inner psychological revolution of the individual. So transformation is only possible in individuals. No society can transform without constant inward revolution—a creative, psychological transformation in the individuals. When individuals transform, it leads the society to transform. So understanding creates its own technique. But the central is not true: technique can never bring about creative understanding.

Limits of Intellect

Reason is a precious value thrown up by evolution and the source of much human progress in culture and civilisation. In the early twentieth century, science studied the objective world and neglected the subjective world. The logical reason, which is the instrument of logic and scientific method felt baffled by the mystery of the external world, and it invaded the citadel of that rationalism. Swami Ranganathananda wrote, "*Vedanta* sees the chief basis of this limitation of scientific reason in its sole dependence on the observed sense data of the external world and neglect of the observer or experience (the subject) of the inner world" (Ranganathananda, 1979). He added, "Reason has to be further developed into a more adequate instrument for pursing the quest for truth."

Swami Vivekananda wrote, "On reason we must have to lay our foundation; we must follow reason as far as it leads; and when reason fails, reason itself will show us the way to the highest plane. Recently many eminent scientists have expressed the limitations of reason or intellect."

Werner Heisenberg wrote, "A rationalistic play with words and concepts is of little assistance here; the must preconditions are honesty and directness. But since *ethics* is the basis for the communal life of men, ethics can only be derived from that fundamental human attitude which I have called the spiritual pattern of the community".

Edwin Hubble said, "The world of pure values, that world which science cannot enter, has no concern whatsoever with probable knowledge. There finality eternal, ultimate truth is earnestly sought."

Max Planck said, "Science means unresting endeavor and continually progressing development toward an aim which the poetic intuition may apprehend, but which the intellect can never fully grasp".

Lincoln Barnett discussed the limitations of the intellect, "All highroads of the intellect, all byways of theory and conjecture, lead ultimately, to an abyss that human ingenuity can never span. For man is enchained by the very condition of his being, his finiteness and involvement in nature. Man is thus his greatest mystery".

Max Born (1949) at the third Pugwash Conference, stated, "Clever, rational ways of thinking are not enough. The danger of mass slaughter can only be overcome by moral conviction, by a determination to replace national prides and prejudices with human love".

Indeed, intellect, ideals, beliefs, concepts, conclusions, knowledge (information), thought structures coupled with feelings and motives are sterile in radical transformation (mutation) of the human psyche, because the whole cannot be approached by the part. All legislation, all reforms of the socio-political-economic system, any tinkering of the time-space matrices, cannot transform the psyche. All education of the intellect or reason has no significance regarding understanding the psycho-dynamics of the conditioned mind-brain-body system.

Psycho-dynamics of the Conditioned Mind-Brain-Body System

Art of Observation

Spencer Brown, in a most spectacular passage explained that the mind in order to see itself "must first cut itself up into at least one state which sees, and at least one other state which is seen". There is energy exchange between the seer (subject) and the seen (object) resulting into distortion of subject and the object; the distorted subject sees the distorted object (non-fact), and distorted subject gets recorded as modified memo, which is analysis, the altering and the adding. So the intellectual approach and analysis are false processes. The objective science also engages itself in intellectual approach and analysis, so it constructs knowledge of a part, which is called relative knowledge.

The quantum revolution was cataclysmic because it challenged the edifice of subject-object dualism. As Sullivan (1949) put it, "We cannot observe the course of nature without disturbing it", or Andrade (1957), "observation means interference with what we are observing—observation disturbs reality" (George Wald, 1988). "The very crux of twentieth century physics is the recognition that the observer cannot be excluded from his observations; he is an intrinsic participant in them". *A Quantum Jump from Symbolic— Dualistic Frame to Non-Dual and Non-Conceptual Frame of Reference.* A scientific mind takes up "the role of a non-concerned observer", in the words of Erwin Schrodinger (1967). When a scientific mode observes a thought, it does not interfere in its flow and does not transfer any energy to thought for its sustenance; the thought blossoms and withers away, which implies that the pseudo-subject goes to abeyance and non-variable attentively takes up the role of true subject. This leads to quantum jump of symbolic-dualistic frame to non-dual and non-conceptual frame of reference of mind spectrum. To be psychologically free and original can only come about when you are aware of your own inward activities, watch what you are thinking and never let one thought escape without observing the nature of it, the source of it. When you begin to see that which is false, then there is the beginning of awareness, of intelligence. You have to be a light to yourself and it is one of the most difficult things in life.

Recent Scientific Discoveries

Modern science has provided experimental evidence that the art of scientific observation (or a mind with scientific temper) leads to ending of subject-object dualism. It implies a quantum jump of symbolic-dualistic frame to non-dual and non-conceptual frame of reference of mind spectrum. The non-dual frame is synergistic to the dualistic frame of mind spectrum; it implies that the non-dual frame is at a higher quantum energy potential of consciousness. The pseudo-subject (recalled memory) goes to abeyance, which leads to ending of subject-object dualism. Erwin Schrodinger (1967) wrote:

'The world is given to me only once, not one existing and one perceived. Subject and object are only one. The barrier between them cannot be said to have broken down as a result of recent experience in the physical sciences, for this barrier does not exist. The world is given but once. Nothing is reflected. The original and the mirror-image are identical. Understanding only the truth can liberate the mind from its ideation; to see the truth, the mind must realise the fact that as long as it is agitated it can have no understanding. The symbolic-dualistic frame is repetitive; it does not have any capacity for understanding; only the non-dual frame can understand the truth. Radical transformation or mutation of the psyche happens when you see the false as the false and the true as the true. This is the basis of right kind of education. Truth is not cumulative. It is from moment to moment."

The word *understanding* implies awareness of the present. The conditioned mind-brain-body system does not have the capacity to perceive the present, so it cannot understand anything. Carl Sagan stated, "We go about our lives understanding almost nothing of the world". Man's capacity for understanding has got blurred. The whole cannot be understood through the part; it can be understood only through intuition (insight) and spontaneity. The humanity is facing this crisis. As the crisis is unprecedented there must also be unprecedented action, which means that the regeneration of the individual must be instantaneous, not a process of time. The answer is embedded in mutation of the human psyche. Understanding is a non-cerebral movement, where the Universal Consciousness, the Divine expresses Itself in a brain that has transcended the cerebral activity, the thought-time structure. Understanding is a movement of the sensitivity, the Intelligence of one's psycho-physical structure. It is a timeless perception. The Unknown has to be discovered, then only it can be understood. Where there is understanding, the Universal Consciousness expresses itself as intuition and spontaneity. Intuition bestows a true meaning of a challenge and it provides its true answer. The answer is called the discovery. The spontaneity bestows the right action. Intuition or insight alone can de-condition the brain.

We cannot understand through effort, through analysis, through comparison, through any form of mental struggle. We cannot understand through motivations, through desire, through attachments. Understanding happens when there is direct embrace of the fact, the awareness. Understanding happens when the original (Intelligence) and the mirror-image (pure perception) arc Identical. It is the intuitive flash that brings understanding.

It is our birthright to grow from the dimension of knowing to understanding. The clarity of understanding is the sunshine of inner Consciousness and living the Truth that one understands gives' a sense of fulfillment. One enjoys the ecstasy of that inner freedom, peace, order, harmony and beauty.

Learning: It is not a result of logical, intellectual argumentation with oneself. When one has the attentiveness of one's own limitations, then an urge for learning the structure and dynamics of mind is born in the mind. When one is not tuned to the chatter of the brain but tuned to the set of frequencies of the fact, then learning is possible. The pain, suffering, sorrow compel one to watch one's mind, which implies a natural and spontaneous desire to learn and live. We have to learn to be open and receptive instead of getting closed. We must jettison the closed system of the successive consciousness and learn to live in an open system of the

Absolute, which implies a flow of energy from the Absolute, to the mind so that the frame of reference makes a quantum jump to a higher quantum energy potential. A frame at a higher quantum energy potential bestows a spontaneous urge for enquiry, to discover the meaning of life, and not to acquire, not to add to memory and store. Learning requires an emptiness from within. Learning requires openness, receptivity and the humility. Learning happens when the object (recalled memory) goes to abeyance, and attentively which takes over as the true subject observes the subjective nature of the fact. As soon as the dualism of subject-object arises, learning ends and the frame gets engaged in information gathering or symbolic-dualistic knowledge. We have come here to learn, learn how to live and to live is to be related in freedom and harmony. Learning is an adventure into the inner realm of mind, it is a willingness to look at life as it is out of inner freedom, out of the state when the past has gone to abeyance. Learning is a movement arising out of an inner freedom, a state of non-identification. There is no accumulation in learning. Learning is the only process where total growth takes place and this is called holistic education, and at every growth there is transformation. Learning results in growth which is defined as decrease of subtle matter content at every moment in the consciousness and growth results in transformation, mutation of human psychology.

Relationship: Relationship is a movement of unfolding what "I am" and not what "I should be". Relationship is a mirror in which one can see oneself. In relationship, there is no place for acquisition, attachment, expectation, suffering. When you feel fulfilled in being what you are and you feel fulfilled in unfolding what you are then the relationships can be non-bargaining, non-acquisitive, non-possessing and there can be harmony of bliss in sharing. The criteria for the new human culture is non-identification functionally, and non-acquisitiveness and non-possessiveness psychologically. We have the responsibility to relate to the self-existing self-consistent, self-evolving, self-sustained life (Universal Consciousness) around us on the one hand and the responsibility to relate to man-made world and the human beings around us on the other hand.

Living is unfolding which is enfolded in us. The very act of unfolding enriches the mind, which implies that the mind makes a quantum jump to a higher quantum energy potential. The act of living with love, without fear will activate and mobilise the perceptive sensitivity, the intelligence. Life moves very fast—ever-renewing, ever-fresh. Each moment can be a fresh communion with the ever-renewing life.

Intuition: Bohm stated, 'The ultimate perception does not originate in the brain or any material structure, although a material structure is necessary to manifest it. The subtle mechanism of knowing the truth does not originate in the brain. Intuition happens in a non-dual frame of reference: it does not originate from the brain, but brain is essential for consciousness to express itself. Intuition or insight is the timeless perception. It is the insight that can recondition the brain, or radical transformation, or mutation of the human psyche. The epistemological revolution leads to mutation of psyche, which implies decrease of matter content in the psyche, which results in higher hierarchical expression of consciousness; and consciousness bestows intuition and spontaneity.

Spontaneity: It implies that there is no psychological time between perception and action. So all action is right. Insight (includes spontaneity) is complete and from that completeness there can be logical, sans, rational action. Only then there can be flowering of the brain and one can have a complete relationship with the mind.

Sensitivity: It is only when we are aware of every movement of our own thought and feeling in our relationship with people, with things and, the Nature, that the mind is open, pliable, not tethered to self-protective demands and pursuits; and only then is there sensitivity to the ugly and beautiful, unhindered by the self, the cultural belief structure. The epistemological revolution bestows higher sensitivity to the mind-brain-body system.

Creativity: Creativeness comes into being when there is constant awareness of the ways of the mind and of the hindrances it has built for itself. Discovery is the beginning of creativeness; and without creativeness, do what we may, there can be no peace or happiness of man (Krishnamoorthy, 1953).

The symbolic-map knowledge is capable of minor inventions, a modification of the old, a use of the old. Discovery is only possible by a non-dual frame of reference of mind spectrum. The epistemological revolution leads to creativeness (Kaur, Singh and Sing, Zoor), which flowers to discovery.

Dualistic and Non-Dualistic Thought

Dualistic thought is a quanta of scattered vibrations. It reflects a reality other than itself, it reflects interactions, and thus it establishes limitations. In the absolute rest frame, a non-dual thought carries out a dance, which is fundamentally its own transcendent nature, true nature. Non-dual thought is a quanta of Fundamental Vibration. When thought truly displays its own inner nature, it is a microcosm of infinity. When thought is consistently able to cease to reflect anything other than itself, at a moment, there is a living enactment of wholeness. When thought arises from the perception of wholeness, it will flow into the feeling of wholeness. At that moment, we say thought is creative; it is a living hollow vibration of the wholeness; it is called intuitive, perceptive of holiness.

Exploration in the Field of the Unknown

Epistemology is the theory of knowing. It implies a quantum jump from intellection to intuition, which may be called epistemological revolution. It is possible that if one lives for a long chronological time in the epistemological revolution, it may get stabilised. It is also possible that in some persons the self-urge may arise to explore further. Those who pursue further exploration, the attentively and the fact coalesce and vanish, and the true Universal Consciousness or Life Field bathes the brain cells. In the brain, the ultimate quantum energy potential of Consciousness presses itself which may be called 'ultimate epistemological revolution'. In philosophy, this state may be called the state of meditation. Meditation is an impersonal happening. This bestows love and compassion.

The ancient seers of India, about 10,000 years ago, perceived a State of true illumination. There is One Reality—the *Unmanifest-Manifested*. The nature of the Unmanifest is Deep silence inactivity (Non-vibration). Passivity, Immutability, Eternal and also Activity (vibration) dynamism and illimitable potency to manifest as many Activity (Active Reality) expresses which is self-hidden in the Silence (Passive Reality).); both are different states of the Supreme Reality, the obverse and converse affirmations; both are Pure Existence and conscious Force, or Self-Existent Bliss and Supreme Intelligence and are One. It is the Active Reality which manifests as the perfect freedom and omnipotence of an eternal divine activity in innumerable galaxies as inanimate world and plant and animal kingdoms.

The Active Reality is a powerful, highly directional, mono-chromatic (same frequency) and coherent (the wave is in one phase) beam of energy; or a state of highest frequency (higher frequency means higher energy), or high quantum energy potential. At the level of man, the intense energy of insight expresses itself as direct perception of the fact, the Reality. The insight acts upon the brain matter and transmutes it, so the brain matter transforms and attains a higher order through insight, or higher quantum energy potential of Consciousness.

Dimensions of Human Life

Man simultaneously lives in two dimensions: (i) the time-space matrices constructed by the mind, the sensual world, the conditioned mind, the known, and (ii) the timeless realm, the Unconditioned mind, the Divine Potential, the Life Field, the Unknown. The mind-brain-body spectrum functions predominantly in two stages:

Stage One: It investigates the psychological mode, where all activity is destructive, leading to a great deal of misery, confusion and sorrow; and the objective scientific mode which investigates the time-space matrices and gives relative knowledge.

Stage Two: The pure religious mode (meditative mode) explores the universal core of religion which deals with the wholeness of life, and bestows absolute perception. In other words, it is exploring the non-cerebral through the non-action of the conditioned mind; it is the growth to a new dimension of consciousness.

Expression of Consciousness

Everything that we experience as material reality [a construct of successive consciousness] is born in an invisible realm beyond space and time [called Universal Consciousness, the Life Field], a realm revealed by science to consist of pure energy. The material reality is at a lower quantum energy potential and information. All objective sciences, social sciences, or any reform to change the external world, cannot bring in any radical transformation in the subjective, the inner, the cultural belief structure. Hence, all education at the intellect level has no significance and basically constructs an illusion.

Sciences now define matter as vibrating and oscillating energy, which has got solidified, the energies acting and interacting with one another. All energies are emanation of Quantum Vacuum Energy (QVE) or Zero-Point Energy (ZPE), or Pure Consciousness, or Life Field Physicists talk of the concept of zero-point energy, or what we call the empty space, the Void, is really a vast ocean of energy. The zero-point energy, or Brahman, or Life Field are analogous.

Every existence, every event in the cosmos and beyond, is an expression of consciousness at a pre-determined hierachical level of expression of consciousness often called immanent quantum energy potential of consciousness. Man alone of terrestrial being has the capacity to enhance his level of awareness, so that the instruments are tuned to higher expression, such as intuition and spontaneity of consciousness. Man has to be a fit channel for the highest quantum energy potential of Universal Consciousness, of Life Field in philosophical language. It is called "a living of man in the Divine and a Divine living of the Spirit in humanity."

Present Education

The psychosocial evolution of man over uncountable aeons have made him an extrovert, which implies awareness of time-space matrices (objective dimension sensual world) and divorcing the inner (subjective dimension suprasensual world) field. In the sensual world, he is engaged in gathering fragmentary knowledge (information) and partial experience and storing this in memory. This has led to his conditioning the psyche, which is heading towards self-annihilation, a race to oblivion.

Man has started living in the psychological dimension of life. There is no such thing as psychological evolution. The present education trains the mind in the continuation of the past and such a mind can never discover the new. The living in the intellect is the way to disintegration. It does not touch the subjective or depth dimension of man, so it is divorced from all eternal values. This cannot lead him to the dimensions of understanding, learning, intuition, spontaneity, creativity, and intelligence, as these are embedded in the subjective dimension of man. Presently, education is a complete failure because it deals with a part. To cultivate efficiency through intellectual pursuits without understanding the wholeness of life, leads to higher entropy and is a pointer to self-destruction and self-annihilation. The chariot of destruction has started moving.

The whole man kind is caught in a crisis of perception or psychic pandemic. All knowledge (information), thought structures, beliefs, concepts, patterns of value education are sterile in transforming (mutation) the human psyche. So all present education has no significance to living, and is absolutely irrelevant to understanding the wholeness of life.

Proposed Education for a Global Society

The world-view implied by modern physics is inconsistent with our present society, which does not reflect the harmonious interrelatedness we observe in nature. We need symbiosis of science and spirituality, or dynamic interplay of new education and individual. We must mobilise the "wheel of *dharma*" in this terrestrial concert we work for "Understanding the Law or the Truth of the Individual".

Modern science, based on its rigorous approach and logical consistency, has brought the subject-object dualism to an 'annihilating edge'. The ending of dualism has awakened the non-dual mode of knowing, therein to perceive the Reality, the Truth of nature direct. It implies that if mind adopts the scientific temper, the subject-object dualism ends. The important experimental observation suggests that we have to introduce Culturing as scientific temper (to understand the objective and the subjective dimensions of man) in colleges and universities. The scientific temper helps to make a quantum jump from symbolic-dualistic frame to non-dual and non-conceptual frame of reference in the mind spectrum; and this quantum jump is called the epistemological revolution. The right kind of education is "An Epistemological Revolution through Scientific Temper".

The epistemological revolution bestows pure perception, which is awareness of the truth, the present, the act, the *what* is. It bestows understanding and learning, intuition and spontaneity, and sensitivity and creativity. It will lead to ending violence, fear and other psychological imbalances. The modern science has provided experimental evidence to the inner world of man, the subjective dimension of man, the omnipresence of Universal Consciousness, the Life Field. Man has to realise here and now that the subjective dimension and the objective dimension of man are a single dynamic flow, a unitary movement. This implies that man has to understand both subjective and objective dimensions of life, or the wholeness of life, and live in the light of that understanding.

When life is anchored in science and spirituality, or objective research and subjective research, there is sanity and balance. When one sees the totality of the outer and the inner, there is perception of the wholeness and out of that perception order arises. Human being has to flower in the symbiosis of science and spirituality. We are today at a truly historic juncture in the long and tortuous history of the human race on Planet Earth. We stand at a bifurcation where one road is leading to Buddha (Wisdom, Intelligence) and the other road to bomb (self-destruction and self-annihilation). Nature is benevolent if man prepares himself to perceive His Grace.

The proposed education will end the action of aggression and assertiveness, it will construct new relationships between individuals or within individuals, and this will end all conflict, pain and misery. The individual will be free from the burden of the past, from the action of will and weight of time—this is the new human being.

We have to undertake the journey to the Sacred Temple of Understanding and Learning, a pilgrimage from psycho-social evolution to spiritual evolution. The fundamentals of the journey are that which attentively purifies the mind and inattentivily adds to pollution. The art of observation leads to a quantum jump to higher hierarchical expression of consciousness, it is a courtesy from the successive consciousness to the Simultaneous Consciousness. A journey to the Temple of Understanding and Learning energizes the new dimension of Simultaneous Consciousness, which is integral and all-inclusive in its nature. This dimension of Consciousness is the only guarantee to ensure survival of mankind and the planet. It is the basis of global education which will lead to the emergence of a new human being who will construct a non-violent and peaceful society.

The future of mankind is embedded in a higher level of awareness, higher level of perception, higher level of sensitivity, higher quantum energy potential of the mind. The journey to the temple of Understanding and Learning is the only global prescription to save mankind from annihilation, to heal our diseased mind-brain-body system and to heal our planet.

The Right Kind of Education

1. Understanding comes only through self-knowledge, which is awareness of one's own total psychological process, or awareness of the psycho-dynamics of the conditioned mind-brain-body system. Each one has to unravel and understand for himself the confusion and disorder of his own nature.

2. The *outer* and the *inner* are one, a unitary, harmonious dynamic movement. Education implies awareness of the dynamic movement of the outer and the inner at every moment. It is awareness of the wholeness of life at every moment. But the

whole cannot be understood through the part. It can be understood only through intuition and spontaneity.

3. Education, in the true sense, is to awaken intelligence/wisdom and love and compassion. It is intelligence that brings order and harmony in the system. Intelligence as the capacity to perceive the true, the present, the fact, the what as, and to awaken this capacity, in oneself and in others, is education.

4. The highest function of education is to bring about an integration of left hemisphere and right hemisphere of the brain to bring about an integrated individual who is capable of dealing with life as a whole.

5. The right education comes with the radical transformation or mutation of the human conditioned psyche. We must learn to seek the Supreme, the Life Field and to learn to live in communion with the laws of nature.

6. Love is not different from truth. Love is that state in which the thought process, as time, has completely ceased. Where there is love there is no problem, and there is complete harmony and order.

7. The foundation of global education is an epistemological revolution through scientific temper. It supports Buddha's proclamation about the need to know the mind, to shape the mind, and to liberate the mind. Buddha said, "Where self is, Truth is not. Where Truth is, self is not". Buddha's words are a challenge for our education.

8. Education must help the child to educate himself. Teach him to look at himself, understand himself. The child can draw out the truth in himself. This gives him the freedom which flowers in his natural growth. Every child is an inquirer, an investigator and a merciless anatomist. He must develop the right scientific temper and then work for understanding of life.

9. Intuition is an assurance and a certitude of the Truth of the individual. There is a 'genius within' us and that expresses or manifests as intuition. Intuition is an opening to the spiritual truth and its power. It bestows a sense of harmony and exactitude for the human being. The highest aim of education is

to perceive the intuition and live in that intuition at every moment. This perfects the physical being to be a perfect instrument for the manifestation of supramental consciousness. He must be a channel of the self-expression of the Divine—a living of man in the Divine and a Divine living of the Spirit in humanity.

Conclusion

The psychosocial evolution of man over uncountable eons have made him an extrovert, which implies awareness of time-space matrices (objective dimension, sensual world) and divorcing the inner (subjective dimension sensual world) field. In the sensual world, he is engaged in gathering fragmentary knowledge (information) and partial experience and storing this in memory. This has led to his conditioning the psyche, which is heading towards self-annihilation, a race to oblivion. The living in the intellect is the way to disintegration. It does not touch the subjective or depth dimension of man, so it is divorced from all eternal values. This cannot lead to understanding, learning, intuition, spontaneity, creativity, and intelligence, as these are embedded in the subjective dimension of man. The world-view implied by modern physics is inconsistent with our present society, which does not reflect the harmonious interrelatedness we observe in nature. We need symbiosis of science and spirituality, or dynamic interplay of new education and individual.

References

1. Fritjof Capra, *The Tao of Physics*, London: Bantam Books (Second Edition), 1988.
2. Federico Mayor Zaragoza, *The Courier*, May 1988, p. 4.
3. Bertrand Russell, *The Impact of Science on Society*, p 77.
4. *Ibid.* p121.
5. Jacques Monod, *Chance and Necessity*, New York: Vintage, 1972.
6. George Wald, in Kishore Gandhi (Ed.), *The Evolution of Consciousness*, New Delhi: National Publishing, 1983, p. 14.

7. Sampooran Singh (Ed.), *The Survival of Mankind and Quantum Jump from Violence to Peace*, New Delhi: Books India International, October 1999, pp. 109-116.

8. Willy Brandt, *The Courier*, op. cit., pp. 29-30.

9. The UNESCO Commission, 1972, in Swami Ranganathananda, *Eternal Values for a Changing Society*, Vol. III, Mumbai: Bharatiya Vidya Bhavan, 1986, pp. 585-87.

10. Sampooran Singh, *Science, Human Values, Value Education and Peace*, New Delhi: NM & NWM, September 1993, pp. xiv + 90.

11. Sampooran Singh, Kaur, Kanwaljit and Singh, Paramjit, *Global Values Education*, Chandigarh: Faith Publishers, January 2001, pp. xii + 116.

12. Sampooran Singh, *An Epistemological Revolution through Scientific Temper*, unpublished manuscript.

13. J. Krishnamurti, *The First and Last Freedom*, London: Victor Gollancz Ltd., 1977, pp, 34-41.

14. Swami Ranganathananda, *Science and Religion*, Calcutta: Advaita Ashrarna, July 1979, p. 109.

15. Swami Vivekananda, in Swami Ranganathananda, *ibid.*, p. 109; Complete Works, Vol. I (eleventh edition), p. 185.

16. Werner Heisenberg, in *Synthesis of Science and Religion*, Mumbai: Bhaktivedanta Institute, June 1988, p. 3.

17. Edwin Hubble, *ibid.*, p. 119

18. Max Planck, *The Philosophy of Physics*, New York: Norton, 1936, p. 83.

19. G.F. Chew, in Gary Zukav, *The Dancing Wu Li Masters*, Fontana/Collins, 1982, p. 331.

20. Lincoln Barnett, *The University and Dr. Einstein*, Mentor Edition, pp. 126-27.

21. Max Born in Hideki Yukawa, *Creativity and Intuition*, Tokyo: Kodansha International Ltd.

22. J,W.N Sullivan, *The Limitations of Science*, New York: Mce ntor Books, 1949, p. 140.

23. E. N da C. Andrade, *An Approach to Modern Physics*, New York: Doubleday Anchor Books, 1957, p. 255

24. George Wald, in *Synthesis of Science and Religion*, Mumbai: The Bhaktivedanta Institute, June 1988, p. 19.

25. Erwin Schrodinger, *What is Life' Mind and Matter*, London: Cambridge University Press, Ed. 1967, p. 128.

26. Ilya Prigogine and Isabella Stengers, *Order Out of Chaos*, Bantam Books, 1984, pp. 5,218

27. Erwin Schrodinger, *op. cit.*, pp. 137, 146.

28. Sampooran. Singh, *The Survival of Mankind and Quantum Jump from Violence to Peace*, op. cit., pp. 111-16.

29. David Bohm, in Gary Zukav, *The Dancing Wu Li Masters*, Fontana/Collins, 1982 (Ed.), p. 327.

30. J. Krishnamurti, *Education and the Significance of Life*, Delhi: B. I. Publication, 1953, pp. 125,127.

31. Kaur, K. Singh, P. and Singh, S. *Science with Creativity*, UK: Ramakrishna Vedanta Centre, November-December 2000, pp. 256-67.

32. Sampooran Singh, Singh, M., Kaur, K. and Singh, P. *God in Science*, Chandigarh: Vishvas Publications Pvt. Ltd., July 1999, pp. 1,2.

33. Sampooran Singh, Kaur, K. and Singh, P., *Global Values Education*, op. cit., p. 97.

34. Sampooran Singh, *Need for Scientific Temper in Value Education; The Right Kind of Global Location: An Epistemological Revolution through Scientific Temper*, unpublished.

35. Lord Buddha, in *The Evolution of Consciousness*, New Delhi: National Publishing House, 1983, p. 239.

36. *Ibid.*, in *The Odyssey of Science, Culture and Consciousness*, New Delhi: Abhinav Publications, 1990, p. 165.

37. Words of Sri Aurobindo and the Mother, *The Right Object of Education*, Pondicherry: All India Magazine, June 2001.

38. In the true sense of the words, "An Epistemological Revolution Through Scientific Temper", or journey to the "Temple of Understanding and Learning", or "Symbiosis of Science and Spirituality" are identical. Similarly, *Universal Consciousness or Life Field or Quantum Vacuum Energy (QVE)*, or *Zero-Point Energy (ZPE)*, or "*Law or the Truth of an individual*, or "*Truth or Law of the Being*", or the "*Spoke of the Dharma*" are identical.

Global Unity in Ancient Indian Education

Shashi Tiwari

It is well recognised that the outlook and methods of education prevalent in a society have a far-reaching significance and influence upon the other social institutions of that society. Education is the principle instrument in the hands of a social group, by means of which it passes on and hands over to the individual and thus to itself the traditions, disciplines and culture it has gathered through long and continual endeavours of the race towards making the best of the human life. Thus, it seeks to train the individual to adjust himself/herself to the ideas and ideals, which have gathered value and respect from the noblest that have made the history of the society. It is evident that amongst all the social institutions, the system of education is of primary significance. Without it all the accumulated knowledge of the ages and all standards of conduct would be lost. The system of education which aims at development of the individual's personality endows him at the same time with the power of rational appreciation. Such a system prevents that conservative and orthodox attitude of mind, which shuns the acceptance of any new idea in the social and moral fields. Real education has value both in so far as it develops the individual personality as well as it socializes the person. The proper idea of education must envisage a coordination of these two aims. Moreover, the development of the personality of individual members of the group will also help the growth of the society.

Ancient Educational System

After this introductory note on the general aims of the education, we may now proceed to the study of nature and grounds of the educational system of ancient Indian thinkers. No nation can be called educated which cannot preserve and expand its cultural heritage. The preservation and spread of national heritage and culture was one of the most important objects of Indian educational system. Besides being a source of illumination and self-fulfillment, it emphasised devotion to social duties and also laid stress on the promotion of happiness of mankind. Steps were taken to realise the ideal of the man/woman/ the society and the humanity. It was declared in *Brahdaranyak Upanishad* that a man can discharge his/her debt to ancestors not merely by procreating sons and daughters but by providing for their proper education as it would benefit future generations. In India, education was treated as a matter of growth, a process of life, which was controlled in its totality.

The survey of education is ancient India may be divided historically in four periods:

1. The first period, from the prehistoric times to 1000 BC
   (*Vedic* age)
2. The second period, from 1000 BC to 200 BC
   (Age of *Upanishads, Sutras* and *Epics*)
3. The third period, from 200 BC to 500 AD
   (Age of the *Dharmas'astras*)
4. The fourth period, from 500 AD to 1200 AD
   (Age of *Puranas* and *Kavyas*) (Altekar, 1957)

The ancient system of education was established on the constant association between the teacher (*Guru*) and the taught (*antevasin*). The function of the teacher (*Acharya*) was to lead the pupil from the darkness of ignorance to the light of knowledge. The Mahabharata as well as the *Ramayana* gives us numerous instances of teachers' very high moral character and learning like *Vishwamitra, Vasistha, Sandipani, Krpacharya* and others. There are references of learned ladies and women teachers in the *Vedas* and *epics*. The words '*Upadhyayani*' and '*Acharyani*' indicate the existence of lady-teachers in that remote past (*Apastamba Grhyadutra* 1.10,11). The ancient educational system evolved its own appropriate method of study. *Kautilya* enumerates the following steps of *Vedic* study: (1) *S'us'ru''a* (listening to the words of the teacher),

(2) *S'ravanam* (grasping the lessons), (3) *Grahanam* (apprehension of the teacher's lecture), (4) *Dharaham* (retention), (5) *Uhapoha* (discussion), (6) *Vijnanam* (full knowledge of the meaning conveyed by the teacher's words), and (7) *Tattvabhinivesa* (comprehension of the underlying truths of the teacher's lessons, Majumdar, 1968).

Ancient educationists considered knowledge (*Vidya*) as the third eye of man/woman which gives him/her insight into all affairs and teaches him/her how to act. According to some, there are four Vidyas or sciences:

1. *Trayi*, the triple *veda*
2. *Anviks'iki*, logic and metaphysics
3. *Danda-niti.* the science of good governance
4. *Vartta*, practical arts such as economics, medicine, agriculture.

Manu adds a fifth *Atma-vidya*, knowledge of soul (*Manusmriti*). The intellectual side of education was developed through the numerous subjects of study referred to. Traditionally, mention is often made in Sanskrit literature of fourteen sciences (*Vidyas*) and sixty-four disciplines of arts and crafts (*kalas*). In short, it can be said that the subjects of study in those days comprised all sorts of knowledge-material and spiritual.

Moral training formed the very pivot and backbone of the educational system and the development of character was the one ideal that dominated it. A set and disciplined life is prescribed for a pupil during education. It is important to note that students were being trained in the habits of simple life, no matter what family they belonged to. Whatever the social position or status of the students' families, they had to take up the same mode of life. In the *Ramayana* and the *Mahabharata*, we find several instances showing how even princes had to undergo the some rigours of the student's life along with their poor fellow students.

Similarity of all and unity among all human-beings is a very general concept inter-woven in the whole of the *Vedic* literature and later Sanskrit scriptures. We find hundreds of passages in the *Vedic* texts mentioning this concept (*e.g., Rigveda* 10.191.2; *Atharvaveda* 3.30 5,7; *Yajurveda* 36.18,40.6). Prayers to the deity are indicative of welfare of all, as mostly they are in plural (*e.g. yajurveda* 3.35, 30.3, *Rigveda* 1.114.10). Brahman is described pervasive in all creatures (*Yajurveda* 32.8). For Him, this whole universe is like a nest (*Yajurveda,* 32.8). The saying of *Yajurveda* reminds the famous *Sanskrit* quotation which means 'this earth is like a family.' Culmination of this concept is indeed the monotheistic doctrine of Indian philosophy. Thus, teaching of global unity was the undercurrent of the *Vedic* wisdom and outlook.

Institution

Generally, there were three types of institutions for the spread of learning during later *Vedic* period. Firstly, there was the normal system under which the teacher, as a settled householder, admitted to his institution pupils of tender age, who left home of their natural parents. This entry into the perceptor's home (Ashrama) was a sort of spiritual birth. They had to live in the premises of the hermitage of the Guru. The Smritis describe rules for the student's residence at the Guru's house. Upanishads speak of the students going to the teacher's places for knowledge. The Mahabharata also describes many hermitages where pupils from distance and different parts of the country gathered for instructions around famous teachers.

Debating circles or Parisads was the second type of educational institution which ministered the needs of the advanced students who improved their knowledge by mutual discussions or by the instruction of literary celebrities and renowned specialists. In the Upanishads, such type of learning could be often noted. *Uddalaka Aruni*, from the *Kuru-Panchala* country, went to the north where in a disputation to which he challenged the northern scholars he had something to learn from their leader *Saunaka* (*Satajatha Brahmana* 11.4.1.2). King *Pravaha Jaivali* was a member of *Panchala Parisad*, an academy of advanced scholars, which he used to attend every morning. *Yajnavalkya* taught his learned wife, *Maitreyi*, by means of a discussion (*Brhadaranyaka Upanisad* 2.4; 4.5).

'Conference' was the third type of institution which developed for the spread of learning in those ancient times. Besides small debates and parisads of localities, there was occasionally summoned by a great king, a national gathering or conference in which scholars or representative thinkers from different parts of the country were invited to exchange their views under royal auspices. The Brhadarayaka Upanishad, the Satapatha Brahmana and the Vayu-Purana had reference of one such conference of Rishi. The king offered a special prize to the person—'the best read', 'the most learned in sacred writ' and 'the wisest'.

Taksas'ila (1500 BC to 180 BC) and *Nalanda* were two famous seats of learning in ancient India which contributed for the cause of global unity at their times. Ramayana and Mahabharata refer to Taksas'ila as a noted centre of learning. The great grammarian Panini hailing from Salatur near Attock and Chanakya, the minister of Chandragupta Maurya are said to have had education in Taksas'ila (Bakshi and Mahajan, 2000). Indian teachers were past masters in the art of explanation and exposition; students from distant countries like Korea and China, Burma and Ceylon, Tibet and Nepal used to brave the dangers of the perilous journey to India to hear the exposition of obscure metaphysical passages which could be heard nowhere else on earth (Mitra, 1964).

The *Jatakas*, sources of historical information, are full of stories giving interesting glimpses of ancient Indian education. Jataka No 252 presents significant details on the system of education and its chief centre Taksasila. "Once upon a time Brahmadatta, king of Banaras, had a son named Prince Brahmadatta. Kings of former times, though there might be a famous teacher living in their own city, often used to send their sons to foreign countries to complete their education, so that they could learn to quell their pride and high mindedness, endure heat or cold, and be made acquainted with the ways of the world". So did this king. He called his son, then sixteen years old, and gave him a pair of one-soled sandals, a sunshade of leaves and a thousand pieces of money with these words, "My son get you to Taksas'ila and study there". This and other Jataka stories show that Taksas'ila was then a prominent centre of learning and education to which flocked scholars from distant parts of India. There were day scholars along with resident pupils. Studies were chosen freely and not according to caste. Taksas'ila offered the highest education in humanities, sciences, arts and crafts, medicine, law, military science and other subjects. Taksas'ila as a centre of higher education, attracted students from far and near, even scholars from distant Greece, if we are to believe in the story of Apollonius of Tyana. According to Jatakas, next to Taksas'ila ranks Banaras as another seat of learning. It was to some extent built up by the graduates of Taksas'ila, who set up there as teachers. Banaras was noted for its school of music also (Mookerji, 1960).

Nalanda, mentioned in the accounts of Hiusen Tsang, was another centre of a truly national character and attracted teachers from the different parts of the country. The Great Masters, *Asanga* and *Vasubandha* were associated with *Nalanda*, as they lived in the latter part of the fifth century AD, when *Nalanda* was already growing up as a centre of education. Mr Pannikar describes that *Darmapaia*, the head abbot of *Nalanda*, at the beginning of the seventh century, was a Tamil noble man from South India; Jiva Mitra, another renowned teacher was from *Andhra* and *S'ilabhadra*, the saintly teacher of Yuan Chwang, was a converted *Brahmana* from the eastern area (*Bakshi* and *Mahajan*, 2000).

The courses of study offered by the *Nalanda* University covered a wide range, almost the entire circle of knowledge then available. They were drawn from the different fields of learning—Brahmanical and Buddhist, sacred and secular, philosophical and practical, sciences and arts. The University at the same time had an international position. Scholars travelled from Indonesia, China, Tibet, Ceylon, Java, Korea and other countries to pay homage to India as their holy land and sent out pilgrims to gather the harvest of her learning and, return home to sow its seeds in a new soil. The outstanding characters in this fruitful cultural intercourse were Fa-Hien, Hiuen Tsang and I-tsing. But there were hosts of other pilgrims to India whose names and achievements are not known to us. There were other pilgrims who had followed Hiuen Tsang and preceded I-tsing during the short interval of only forty years. They were Thonmi, Hiuen Chin, Taouhi, Hwui Lu, Tang, Taou-sing,

Aryavarman, Buddhadharma, all of whom sought Indian wisdom as students of *Nalanda* as its chief centre and repository. In the same (seventh) century, we have also to record the visits of the Chinese monks, Ou-kong and Ki-ye to *Nalanda* (Bakshi and Mahajan, 2000). This cultural interaction between these Asiatic countries and India was not one-sided. The students of *Nalanda* took the lead. *Nalanda* scholars worked in China and Tibet mostly for academics in Buddhism.

Thus, scholars flocked to *Nalanda* to complete their studies, and at the same time went abroad from *Nalanda* for spreading the message of wisdom. *Nalanda's* contribution to knowledge is an evidence of global unity in ancient education system. Among other known ancient Indian Universities, *Valabhi, Vikrams'ila, Jagaddala, Odantapuri, Mithila* and *Nadia* were important. The scholars trained by these centres distinguished themselves by their work in foreign countries. Indian scholars played prominent part in introducing Indian thought to China. Thus, these centers were developed as excellent examples of global unity in the educational system of ancient India.

Conclusion

The above review of the salient features of the ancient educational system will prove sufficient to impress upon our minds how it functioned as a social organisation, calculated to create strong personalities, whose reason was sought to be kept ever awake, whose mental powers and capacities were well-developed, whose understanding of the meaning of life, in general and in detail, was founded on a broad basis. India's liberal educational system wielded great influence on the growth of socio-cultural thought. We may close this paper with the following quotation from the S'atapatha Brahmana, which quite admirably sums up the main virtues and aims of education as conceived by the ancient Indians:

"Now, then, in praise of learning: learning and teaching are a source of pleasure to man; he becomes ready minded, or mentally well-equipped and independent of others and day-by-day, he acquires prosperity. He sleeps peacefully, he is the best physician for himself; and (peculiar) to him are restraint of the senses, delight in steadiness of mind, development of intelligence, fame and last but not the least in importance, the task of perfecting the people (*Satapatha Porabwana* 11.5.7.1)

References

1. Altekar A.S., *Education in Ancient India*, Banaras : Anand Kishore, 1951
2. Bakshi, S.R. and Mahajan, *Lipi Education in Ancient India* (edited), Delhi: Deep and Deep 2000, p.58
3. Majumdar R.C. *The Age of Imperial Unity*, Bombay : Bharatiya Vidya Bhavan, 1968, pp. 583-84
4. Mitra, Veda, *Education in Ancient India*, Delhi: Arya Book Depot, 1964
5. Mookerji R.K., *Ancient Indian Education*, Delhi: Motilal Banarsidass, 1960.

Values in the Context of
School Education in India

J.S. Rajput

The 21st century inherited unparallel multifaceted growth and development of the 20th century. Space was conquered, and human capacities challenged and even overcome by computers. Apartheid and colonialism vanished. The concept of global village became visible. The denizens of the globe became neighbours. Human drudgeries were reduced. So much more could be said on the brighter side (Venkataraman, 2002). Unfortunately there is an extremely dark side as well. 23% of the world's population is still living in extreme poverty. Primary school enrolments still stand at 84%. The richest 5% of the world's population have incomes 114 times more than that of the poorest 5%. Everyday more than 30,000 children around the world die of preventable diseases. In Botswana, more than a third of adults suffer from HIV/AIDS (UNDP, 2002). And the list just can't be exhaustive.

The diversities, particularly the gap between the rich and the poor, have not reduced. In some sense several of these have increased. Illiteracy and ignorance continue to support exploitation and sub-human living. Nearly a quarter of world's population remains hungry. Nearly three quarters of world resources are still cornered by less than a quarter of the people. Democracies have apparently been strengthened. Communism has withered away. But the issues of equality even amongst sovereign nations remain elusive. The global village in reality could make every human being a neighbour of everyone else. Are we really becoming evolved human beings who would not only live in the neighbourhood but also become neighbourly?

The preceding century gave great hopes to people particularly in the countries, which were exploited by alien masters for centuries and were often designated as colonies, underdeveloped nations or as developing countries. Some of them have been able to respond effectively to the hopes, expectations and aspirations of their citizens. In majority of the cases, people stand disillusioned. Democracies, quite often taken over by military regimes have brought corruptions and exploitations in different forms and formats. Those who were suffering earlier continue to suffer more and perhaps in more ways.

Twentieth century was the first time ever that Universal Elementary Education was discussed globally and every nation resolved to strive to achieve this goal. Educational expansion has been an unparalleled phenomenon. The challenge still remains enormous in proportion and magnitude. The war against poverty, unemployment, exploitation and ill-health often gets relegated to background as the battle of political egos, mutual distrust, religious differences, bigotry and fanaticism looms large globally at one place or other. The world, in spite of all the advances, achievements, resolutions and resolves remains an unpeaceful and violent place to live in. Millions of refugees and victims of violent conflicts have probably one question to ask—why have all the progress and growth been so mechanical, materialistic and self-centered? What has happened to the basic human instinct of 'love thy neighbour'? Why have human beings slowed down in growing up spiritually? What has happened to moral, ethical and humanistic values preached by every civilisation everywhere from times immemorial? Efforts to establish inter-faith dialogues, initiatives towards nurturance and inculcation of values and efforts to make people learn 'how to live together' are not bearing much visible fruits. How could one delineate strategies as to the causes and the reasons for such inhuman rather anti-human developments?

I had two unique opportunities to interact with a large number of teachers, teacher educators, educationists, parents and enlightened citizens throughout the country during the last decade of the 20th century. Initially, it was the nation-wide process of consultation with the different groups of stakeholders in education to develop a curriculum framework for teacher education in India. It was released in August, 1998. Subsequently, it was a similar but more intensive process of consultation to develop the curriculum framework for school education for the initial years of the twenty first century for the country. Everywhere, practically in every discussion and interaction, one single issue emerged most prominently in different forms: What has happened to values? Why education is not contributing towards inculcation, nurturance and development of values? If education would not accept this challenge who else would?

Education systems obviously have a responsibility. There are innumerable instances and examples of the same everywhere. I came across a book in The NCERT library titled "Spirituality in Elementary Schools", planned in 1945 and published in 1947. The Principals Association of United States of America, Washington, DC published it. It contains contributions from the Principals of Schools on how they were making attempts to bring in spirituality in their programmes and practices in schools. Teachers of the then victorious nation were probably not content with a victory in the war alone. Though they knew it was a big achievement but human beings need bigger achievements and these can only come through proper nurturance of spiritual values and spirituality. Globally, every nation is concerned and is paying attention to values in life and the need to understand and internalise spirituality. But, in India, the land of multi-religions, at the end of 20th century, a handful of intellectuals are raising reservations about the proposition made to the nation that India needs a system of education, which should not ignore spirituality and inculcation of values.

In Indian context, the post-independent period, though preceded by Gandhian influence and values, has witnessed gradual erosion of essential moral, social and cultural values. The disregard for value system is wide-spread. In practical terms, the potential of the value-based system to contribute to the growth of the nation and its citizens almost stands ignored. The race for materialistic gains has obliterated pursuits of spirituality and human values, which have been characteristics of Indian ethos and psyche. Teachers were supposed to be embodiments of knowledge as well as practitioners of moral and spiritualistic values. As Acharyas, they were supposed to be the role models not only for young children but also for the entire community. They were supposed to nurture the young generations in their own manner and style, and prepare almost everyone to attempt and realise the ultimate purpose of human life, while living a good quality life in the community. Schools could develop as the nurseries for value inculcation, value development and value nurturance. It was also expected that value education would lead to self-recognition which in turn would facilitate the spiritual march from the level of sub-consciousness to that of super-consciousness through the different intermediary stages (NCERT, 2000).

Perceptions about the teachers and expectations from teachers have also changed over the last five decades. The teacher-community relationship has undergone a downward slide. The environment external to school education has created its impact on not only the way the education system functions but also on the very approach and attitude of teachers. In spite of such temporary distortions, the nation still looks towards its teachers with great expectations. The country needs value enriched citizens. Education can contribute most substantially. People still expect that value-based education would help the nation fight against all kinds of fanaticism, ill-will, violence, disharmony, corruption, exploitation and mutual hatred.

Indian society has generally derived its values from the religions of the peoples of India. Indian state is secular but the society is religious. This, in fact, supports and augments secularism. Perhaps school alone could be able to achieve the dream of Gandhi, as quoted by Palkhivala (1994):

"Gather together under one banner all men from all religions and races of India and infuse into them the spirit of solidarity and oneness to the utter exclusion of all communal and *parochial* sentiments."

"By religion, I do not mean formal religion, or customary religion, but that religion which underlies all religions, which brings us face to face with our Maker."

For Gandhiji, all religions were different roads converging towards the same point. Hence following a particular road was immaterial and a personal choice so long as the goal was the same. His goal was an ordered moral government of the universe. He always maintained that to him 'religion should pervade everyone of our actions'. He highlights his perception on several occasions (Palkhivala, 1994):

"The need of the moment is not one religion, but mutual respect and tolerance of the devotees of the different religions. We want to reach not the dead level, but unity in diversity. The soul of religions is one, but it is encased in a multitude of forms. The latter will persist to the end of time". At one stage, India again needed to free itself from the alien yoke. Today, it needs leaders of the people with commitment, dedication and devotion at the level of the leaders of pre-independence era. Gandhiji inspired majority of them. 'My life is my message', said Gandhi and India understood it. The Gandhian thinking underscores several recommendations of the Education Commission. The same inspiration has led the National Curriculum Framework to state:

"Another significant factor that merits urgent attention now is religion. Although it is not the only source of essential values, it certainly is a major source of value generation. What is required today is not religious education but education about religions, their basics, and the values inherent therein and also a comparative study of the philosophy of all religions"(NCERT, 2000).

Why do our own people undermine Indian achievements and contributions to human civilisation? This can be understood only when one refers to the genesis of the inherited system of education. To do so, one has to go back to the proclamation of Macaulay's minutes of 1835. The approach advocated by Macaulay and its subsequent impact is now well known to teachers and educationists. Macaulay did not have any faith in the indigenous Indian literature and knowledge. It is another matter that *vidya*, *shiksha, jyana, taleem, ilm* have always been in the forefront of Indian thought, action and deed.

Macaulay minutes state, "intellectual improvement of the people has to be the main task of East India Company." It further observes, "the Dialects commonly spoken among the natives of this part of India contain neither literary nor scientific information and are, so poor and rude that, until they are enriched from some other quarters, it will not be easy to translate any valuable work into them". He is very clear about his perceptions: "I am quite ready to take the oriental learning at the valuation of orientalists themselves. I have not found one among them who could deny that single shelf of a good European library was worth the whole native literature of India and Arabia. The intrinsic superiority of the western literature is, indeed, fully admitted by those members of the committee who support the oriental plan of education." Macaulay goes on to add: "What we spend on Arabic and Sanskrit is not merely a loss to the cause of truth, it is bounty money paid to raise up champions errors. Assuredly it is the duty of the British Government in India to be not only tolerant but neutral on all religious questions." Macaulay further expressed, "We must at present do our best to form a class who may be interpreters between us and the millions whom we govern, a class of persons, Indian in blood and colour, but English in taste, in opinion, in morals, and in intellect."

Macaulay's policy has yielded the intended result. A small group of persons have assigned themselves a new role to thrust their own definition of secularism on the nation. Secularism to them means: Religion is to be discarded and disregarded in thought, action and deed. Their present dictum is—'None can mention religion in any form in schools, we are secular!' Amazing, some of them also declare themselves to be the only custodians of the legacy of Gandhi. However, when one peruses the Gandhian ideas, one is confronted with his clarity, vision, perception, and universality. Unfortunately, some have misinterpreted his views. Several existing problems are the consequence of the same.

Basic Values

In India, achieving social cohesion and national integration and nurturing the ethos of learning to live together have to be the prime objectives of education at this juncture. Needless to say the world needs more enlightened citizens tomorrow. Most substantial contribution to the same would come from good quality education. This is recognised and acknowledged world over. *Satya, Dharma, Shanti, Prem* and *Ahimsa* have been preached consistently by the sages and seers, by the saints and sufis in the continuity of Indian culture, tradition and heritage. Satya has been acknowledged as the highest religion, *Dharma* encompasses righteousness, nobility and exemplary *aacharan*. Nani Palkhivala elaborates Shanti as 'the calm of the mind, the serenity, inner peace and total stability within yourself which alone enables you to possess your soul before you die'. He further envisions *Prem* as 'the greatest force in the world for which there has never been a substitute in the past nor would be in future'. It is so well embedded in the Indian ideal of 'Vasudhaiva Kutumbakam'. Regarding *Ahimsa*, J. Robert Oppenheimer wrote in 'Einstein: A Centenary Volume':

"Einstein is also, and I think rightly, known as a man of very great goodwill and humanity. Indeed, if I had to think of a single word for his attitude towards human problems, I would pick the Sanskrit word *Ahimsa*, not to hurt, harmlessness" (Palkhivala, 2000).

A few people have apprehensions about the renewed emphasis on values in school education and the need to make children aware of the basics of all religions of the people of India. For them, it is against secularism. Can such a high level of philosophical thought, resulting out of contemplation, meditation and search be ignored by anyone? India needs to unearth what it has achieved much earlier than others in knowledge, wisdom and spirituality.

The present need is to enable the learner to acquire knowledge and skills to develop concepts and inculcate values commensurate with social, cultural, economic and environmental realities at the local, national and universal levels. The social values, aimed at friendship, co-operation, compassion, self-discipline, courage and love, for social justice have to be internalised. Truth, righteous conduct (*Dharma*), peace, love and non-violence form the core universal values for every one and none can have any dispute about it, no matter whatever be the pluralities and diversities of different kinds.

Experts are also of the opinion that different values need to be integrated at different levels of education, starting from primary stage itself. Necessary precautions have also been highlighted as a word of caution. 'Education about religions must be handled with extreme care. All steps must be taken in advance to ensure that no personal prejudice or narrow minded perceptions are allowed to distort the real purpose of this venture and no rituals, dogmas and superstitions are propagated in the name of education about religions. All religions therefore have to be treated with equal respect (*Sarva Dharma Sambhava*) and that there has to be no discrimination on the ground of any religion (*Panthnirapekshata*)'.

Educationists, teachers, teacher educators who understand the present educational needs, have suggested the inclusion of certain aspects for emphasising the need to develop key qualities like regularity, punctuality, cleanliness, self-control, industriousness, willingness to serve, creativity, sensitivity to equality, fraternity and others. This is a treasure that India has discovered in spirit, spirituality, *dharma*, knowledge and wisdom long ago but still remains untapped and unused. Children surely deserve an education rooted in the composite culture of the country, which is committed to progress. Nani Palkhivala (2000) very well illustrates it:

"It has been my long-standing conviction that India is like a donkey carrying a sack of gold—the donkey does not know what it is carrying but is content to go along with the load on its back. The load of gold is that fantastic treasure - in arts, literature, culture, and some sciences like *Ayurvedic* medicine—which we have inherited from the days of the splendour that was India. Adi Sankaracharya called it "the accumulated treasure of spiritual truths discovered by the Rishis." Rabindranath Tagore said, "India is destined to be the teacher of all lands."

Needless to say that after a period of nearly 3000 years of highest level of intellectual contributions in these areas, there was a period of decline but the spirit never vanished. Sri Aurobindo predicted that India would be the moral leader of the world:

"The Indians must have the firm faith that India must rise and be great and that everything that happened, every difficulty, every reverse must help and further their end... The morning was at hand and once the light had shown itself, it could never be night again. The dawn would soon be complete and the sun rises over the horizon. The sun of India's destiny would rise and fill the entire India with its light and overflow India and overflow Asia and overflow the world. Every hour, every moment could only bring them nearer to the brightness of the day that God has decreed."

Essentially the first and foremost value which inspired the philosophy of education in Ancient India was that of the quest for liberation of the individual from the bondage of evil (NCERT, 2002). The second simultaneous value is that of tolerance or forbearance and the third is the fundamental principle of Nishkama Karma, devotion to duty without expectations. Every generation expectedly should be the inheritor of the wisdom and experience of preceding ages and of people. Education should contribute in this understanding, appreciation and analysis and take away the individual from narrow and selfish ends. Identification of the objectives of life comes through the value of compassion. A symphony of self, society and nature prepares him to serve, to change and to contribute to the change for the good of others. Can education set aside its responsibility to nurture the individual, empowering him/her to achieve harmony within himself/herself and with the world outside? Education lights the path of spirituality and in fact is so accepted by the world religions. Education prepares the human beings to strengthen their inner strength that enable them to face the joys and sorrows, tragedies and treasures with dignity and grace. It eventually leads to the search of immortality. No better description of the objectives of education could be there than the one made in Brihadaranyaka Upanishad in the prayer:

> *"Asato ma sadgamaya*
> *Tamaso ma jyotirgamaya*
> *Mrityor ma amritam gamaya."*
> *Lead us from the unreal to the Real*
> *Lead from darkness into Light*
> *Lead from death unto Immortality.*

Key Elements

Educationists and stakeholders need to examine whether our educational system really prepares children to have an integral view of life. Never before we had such resources and support to gather more information, more facts and more knowledge as today. Have we really become wiser also as human community? Why have we not won over narrow considerations, trivialities of differences, which lead to inhuman strategies and insufferable pain of innumerable human beings? To understand and appreciate the situation, it would be necessary to understand the significance of humanistic, cultural, ethical and moral values. A peripheral analysis of visible conflicts alone would not give lasting solutions. These are the days when it is often said that a political solution is much better than a military solution. Probably no political solution could be ever lasting as politics is quite unpredictable. It is the value, which persists and upgrades, energizes and nurtures wisdom. That alone could give solutions to the problems created by human beings themselves, the consequences of which they themselves suffer most. Social values and social structures are influenced by the changes; moral standards also take new forms and shapes. However, the moral, social and cultural values remain prominent and that alone provides support base to the social structures. The pace of change often creates confusion among societies and communities, which are usually attuned to taking a slow view of the changes. Probably we have to adopt a fast track strategy everywhere, including education and prepare to run on the same to ensure that our system do not lag behind in the race for a better quality of life.

Perceptions on the need, nature and necessity of value education in schools are primarily drawn from the National Policy on Education, 1986. It takes note of the growing concern over the erosion of essential values and the increasing cynicism in the society. Curriculum renewal and development needs to respond to this situation. (Education is universally accepted as a forceful tool for cultivation of social, ethical, moral and humanistic values.) The National Policy on Education also takes note of the fact that in a culturally plural society one has to be extremely cautious in approach and conscious of the sensitivities before embarking upon a programme of development and nurturance of values. In a secular society, education should foster universal and eternal values oriented towards unity and integration of people and targeting to achieve social cohesion and understanding. The Policy highlights and expects value education to help eliminate obscurantism, religious fanaticism, violence, superstition and fatalism. In addition, it expects a combative role, which value education has to perform in making people familiar with the rich cultural heritage and the composite culture of India, the Indian thought and approach to national and universal goals and perceptions. Needless to say, these are high expectations and pose a great challenge primarily before school education system. It can no longer ignore any of these aspects or expectations.

School Education

It is true that schools and educational systems are not isolated islands. They can't remain untouched by the prevailing mood of indifference and even disregard to the entire value system. To say the least, value system is crumbling in practically every aspect of human endeavour and ingenuity. At the same time, the task of guiding the nation and the national psyche has traditionally been the responsibility of the educational system, particularly of teachers. Consequently, the present systems of school education, in whatever shape and condition it is, has to accept the challenge and strive to restore and sustain the universal and eternal values oriented towards the unity and integration of the people, their moral and spiritual growth. It has to prepare them to unearth the 'treasure that lies within them'. It has been beautifully enunciated, elaborated and expanded by the Delors Commission Report entitled "Learning: The Treasure Within". No system of education can neglect the fact that every human being need to grow spirituality and develop capacity to ask the question 'who they are, and what is the ultimate purpose of human life'. Only a proper value-oriented education would facilitate their spiritual march from the level of sub-consciousness to that of super-consciousness through different intermediary stages. The war against fanaticism, violence, dishonesty, avarice, corruption and exploitation, fatalism and other ills can never be won unless and until a strong base of values get internalised by a large number of citizens, if not by all.

One of the foremost values is the need for strengthening the national identity and promoting national integration. Towards this the Constitution of India enshrined certain basic values. These were identified as core components of the curriculum in the National Policy on Education, 1986. They remain valid in much greater magnitude on each passing day. These are: The history of India's freedom movement; The Constitutional obligations; the content essential to nurture national identity; India's common cultural heritage; egalitarianism, democracy and secularism; equality of sexes; protection of the environment; removal of social barriers; observance of the small family norm, and inculcation of scientific temper.

The Fundamental Duties as laid down in Article 51A of Part IVA of the Indian Constitution, also have to be included in the core components. These are to: (a) abide by the Constitution and respect its ideals and institutions, the National Flag and the National Anthem;   (b) cherish and follow the noble ideals which inspired our national struggle for freedom; (c) uphold and protect the sovereignty, unity and integrity of India; (d) defend the country and render national service when called upon to do so; (e) promote harmony and the spirit of common brotherhood among all the people of India, transcending religious, linguistic and regional or sectional diversities; (f) to renounce practices derogatory to the dignity of woman; (g) value and preserve the rich heritage of our composite culture; (h) protect and improve the natural environment including forests, lakes, rivers, wild life and to have compassion for the living creatures; (i) develop the scientific temper, humanism and the spirit of enquiry and reform; (j) safeguard public property and abjure violence, and (k) strive towards excellence in all spheres of individual and collective activity so that the nation constantly rises to higher levels of endeavour and achievement (NCERT, 2000).

The issue of core elements and fundamental duties needs to be viewed comprehensively and in synergy. The two are intertwined and inter-linked. The relationship of human rights and human duties is best illustrated by an anecdote from the life of Mahatma Gandhi. It is said that Gandhiji was consulted by the UNESCO in finalizing the draft of the Charter on universal declaration of human rights. Gandhiji, it is said, wrote back that his illiterate but wise mother had advised him much earlier in life that everyone must do his duty so that others can get their rights. I have never seen a more forceful statement than this on the power of values internalised and inculcated at childhood. This one simple statement in appropriate elaboration could become the beacon light for value education in schools.

To achieve this, India needed its own system of education. Mahatma Gandhi very well summarised Macaulay's minutes and the resulting disaster in his famous speech of 1931.

"That does not finish the picture. We have the education of this future state. I say without fear of my figures being challenged successfully, that today India is more illiterate than it was fifty or a hundred years ago, and so is Burma, because the British administrators, when they came to India, instead of taking hold of things as they were, began to root them out. They scratched the soil and began to look at the root, and left the root like that, and the beautiful trees perished. The village schools were not good enough for the British administrator, so he came out with his programme. Every school must have so much paraphernalia, building, and so forth. Well, there were no such schools at all. There are statistics left by a British administrator which show that, in places where they have carried out a survey, ancient schools have gone by the board, because there was no recognition for these schools, and the schools established after the European pattern were too expensive for the people, and therefore they could not possibly overtake the thing. I defy anybody to fulfill a programme of compulsory primary education of these masses inside of a century. This very poor country of mine is ill able to sustain such an expensive method of education. Our state would revive the old village school master and dot every village with a school both for boys and girls."

Initiatives

Even prior to Gandhiji, Indian luminaries of freedom struggle strove to enlighten the Indians about their own knowledge, scholarship, achievements and contributions of the past. These included Swami Dayanand (1825-83), Dadabhai Naoroji (1825-1917), Bal Gangadhar Tilak (1856-1920), Gokhale (1866-1915). Contemporary thinkers like Rabindranath Tagore (1861-1941), Sri Aurobindo (1872-1950), Dr. Zakir Hussain (1897-1969) worked in this direction. Various institutions were established and strategies evolved towards developing character and commitment and internalise values among the citizens. Gandhiji's Nai Taleem had very important component of value education. Values emphasised were cooperation, dignity of labour, simple living and sharing.

After independence almost all the committees and commissions have emphasised the need for value education. Some of the important milestones in value education have been the recommendations of University Education Commission (1948-49), Secondary Education Commission (1952-53), Shri Prakash Committee (1961), Education Commission (1964-66) and National Commission on Teachers (1983). The Standing Committee of the Parliament has made some very bold and practical recommendations for Ministry of Human Resource Development under the Chairmanship of Shri S.B. Chavan. Its report was presented to the Parliament of India in February 1999. Its recommendations on value education and religion have been included comprehensively in the Curriculum Framework for School Education published in November 2000. It is also relevant to note that the Committee on the teaching of fundamental duties to the citizens of India submitted its report in the year 1999. The two documents together emerge as the manifestations of nation's concern on human rights, duties and values. The absence of these three is eroding the body politic of the nation. The maximum suffering is inflicted upon Gandhiji's 'last man'. One may hasten to add that practically everyone suffers when values get eroded. We are experiencing this scenario in India. It is in spite of the fact that at the policy level education system in India consistently emphasizes the need to integrate values in all aspects of school education. Somehow at the implementation stage the policy formulations have not been transformed into pragmatic strategies.

Globally, India is recognised as the 'Guru' in spiritual understanding and appreciation. There is a growing concern on some kind of indifference that exists in the educational system towards basic values in the post-independence period. The understanding of basic tenets of the religions of the people of India in right spirit is essential for social cohesion and mutual respect. This makes it imperative for the school curriculum to include inculcation of basic values and an awareness of all the major religions of the country as a curricula component.

Approaches in Value Education

One more model, which has been put to practice at several places, consist of value education being taught as a separate subject with a different curriculum and a different teacher. Those who are inclined towards this approach have provided for a school programme for the same and they strive hard to develop specific textual materials. This contradicts the dictum that values cannot be taught but they can only be caught.

The Second model is the judicious integration of the identified values with all the subjects of study in the scholastic areas and all the activities and programmes in the co-scholastic areas. Educationists, teachers, teacher educators and other stakeholders within education endorse the value-integrated curriculum. This has emerged during the nation wide consultations during the past two years. Through such an approach, the goals and objectives of value inculcation could be achieved in the classrooms, in the playgrounds, in cultural programmes, community interaction and such other activities. The National Curriculum Framework for School Education proclaims:

"A comprehensive programme of value inculcation must start at the very earliest stage of school education as a regular part of school's daily routine. The entire educational process has to be such that the boys and girls of this country are able to know 'good', love 'good' and do 'good' and grow into mutually tolerant citizens. The comparative study of the 'philosophies' of religions can be taken up at the secondary and higher secondary stages" (NCERT, 2000).

The integrated approach also considers every teacher as a teacher of values, every curriculum development as a value development. It acknowledges that every subject of the activity provides scope for the same.

In the Indian context, several voluntary agencies and other institutions have developed their own models and approaches of value inculcation, development and nurturance. Their success depends upon the commitment of those who initiate, expand and extend. The response may range from full acceptance or indifference or total alienation. Some parents and schools may be very enthusiastic. Others may not be so enthusiastic but, even they would like the best of values to be nurtured and internalised.

This is the time to focus on values in education more prominently than ever before. Evolving suitable and result oriented strategy for implementation is to be accepted as the joint responsibility of the school, the teacher and the community. All of them need to work together. This trinity can seek guidance and support from other sources as well. Eventually, it is the level of their internalisation of the goals and objectives and their personal commitment that would matter. An institution could consider using some of the following as inputs to a comprehensive integrated strategy for value inculcation (Rajput, 1999):

- A critical look at the curricular materials from the point of view of potentialities and possibilities of utilising each one of these for value enrichment with suitable changes in the teaching-learning strategies would need no extra time and result in no additional curriculum load;

- Continuous review of co-curricular and extra-curricular activities which could help in value education through participating, experiencing, working, playing and learning together. These could create great impact on individual learners, particularly in broadening their approach and attitudes towards life;

- A large number of persons and groups work selflessly for the deprived and downtrodden and serve others. Interaction with them could really create perceptible impacts;

- Utilisation of available folklore, national monuments, forms of folk culture and indigenous expertise to imbibe a sense of belonging and pride. This could be attempted in every place by every alert teacher;

- Environment, energy, pollution, population and such other issues could be the talking points in seminars and discussions amongst the peers. Invited experts could assist these;

- Utilisation of community resources and expertise through intensive interaction; making the community realise that the institution belongs to them could lead to several value related activities;

- Providing interaction opportunities with persons of unimpeachable character, sacrifice, creative abilities, literary tastes or scholarly attitudes, whose mere presence motivate others;

- Developing an interactive environment in the institution that nurtures the urge for more knowledge, scholarship, learning and willingness to take responsibilities. Participatory programmes like dances, drama, debates or sports, in which both the staff and the students participate could enliven the atmosphere. All functions, programmes, celebrations, gatherings need to ensure that no group or community feels neglected or isolated;

- Make the institutions responsive to emergencies like floods, fire, drought, etc. This would strengthen mutual relationship with the society;

- Visits to institutions, establishments, centers of creative arts, zoos, museums and homes for the aged and handicapped not only to enhance knowledge and understanding, but also generate appreciation and empathy;

- Cleanliness within the institution helps, in a big way. Development of aesthetic sensibilities is a basic imperative of individual preparation;

- Examples from social life of the institutions and community that reinforce human aspects of individual efforts and group efforts need to be disseminated and discussed. These create a lasting impression.

Task Ahead

The strength of the bond between the teacher and the learner is critical not only to the process of teaching and learning but also to the growth of the two. Teacher acts as the catalyst in developing the skills of thinking, observing, interpreting and inferring amongst the pupils. Teacher's role extends far beyond the mere transmission of information or helping children prepare for higher scores in public examinations. The eternal expectations from the teacher-pupil relationship is that it would lead to full development of the latter's personality. It still remains high in the psyche of every community. The basic seeds of eternal values are sown in early stages. The school and the teacher nurture them. The family assists the process. For every teacher to become a teacher of values, certain basic inputs must become critical components of the teacher preparation processes. Only those committed to lifelong learning, filled with curiosity, equipped with scientific temper, willing to acknowledge their mistakes and having an open mind could really think of becoming such teachers. Only they would receive love, affection and respect from their students. The entire process of teacher education, which has remained rather stagnant for decades, needs to identify the challenges before it and prepare to respond to these without any delay. While professional competence is essential, more essential is the inculcation of that diminishing quality, the commitment amongst teachers. It could be seen as commitment to the learner, to the community, to the profession, to excellence and to values. Preparation of and support to good quality teachers must remain the top priority in any initiative for value inculcation and development. The issues like recruitment procedures, initial education, in-service education of teachers and avenues for their professional growth and development deserve a fresh approach and a dynamic attitude.

Confucius, when asked whether it was necessary to serve gods, replied, "you do not know how to serve your fellowmen; how can you serve gods?" Swami Vivekanand exhorted, " If you want to serve God, serve men". Schools need to prepare pupils who would serve others.

References

1. Venkataraman R: *Religion and 21st Century*, Aryan Heritage, Volume XX No. 175, New Delhi: D.A.V. College Managing Committee, 2002.
2. UNDP, *Human Development Report*, New Delhi: Oxford University Press, 2002.
3. NCERT, *National Curriculum Framework for School Education*, New Delhi, 2002.
4. NCTE, *Curriculum Framework for Quality Teacher Education*, New Delhi, NCTE, 1998.
5. UNESCO, *Learning: The Treasure Within*, Paris: UNESCO, 1996.
6. Palkhivala N.A., *Essential Unity of all Religions*, Bombay: Bharatiya Vidya Bhawan, 1994.
7. Palkhivala N.A., *India's Priceless Heritage*, Bombay: Bharatiya Vidya Bhawan.
8. Rajupt J.S., *Education in a Changing World: Forces and Fallacies*, New Delhi: Vikas Publishing House, 1999.
9. Rajput J.S.: *Dimensions of Curriculum Change*, New Delhi: NCERT, 2002.
10. Rajput, J.S. (Ed): *Symphony of Human Values: A Collection by* J.S. Rajput, New Delhi: NCERT, 2002.

Value Education for Global Society

Contribution of Bharatiya Vidya Bhavan

J. Veeraraghavan

In dealing with value oriented education, there are two issues that educators have to plan for. One relates to the timeless, and eternal struggle between good and evil. This constant struggle arises internally in our minds and externally in the world. As the famous Hindi Poet Jayashankar Prasad observed: "It is a struggle between Devas and Danavas, which has been there always and will go on". The Bhagvat Gita also says that whenever there is a great deal of adharma or injustice, God manifests himself to tackle the same.

Value Education

Educators have to play a fundamental role in enabling their students, whether children or adults, to distinguish between good and evil and stand for with good and against evil. This is' education leading to capability building in moral discrimination. There is wide range of moral standards obtaining in students, just as there is wide range of intelligence. Educationists provide for handling the brilliant ones as well as those with low IQ (slow learners) and have different strategies for different levels of intelligence. In the same way, one must provide for value oriented education for those who are low on the moral scale and also for those who are high on the scale. The educators role is to inculcate eternal values irrespective of the current level of moral standards obtaining in the students.

While the struggle between good and evil may be eternal and timeless, it is also a fact that there has been a general progress of civilisation with good often triumphant over evil. One would agree with Shri Aurobindo that there is a gradual and progressive descent of the Divine in the universe around us resulting in continuous improvement of human condition. The Hindi Poet, Dinkar stated in his epic poem "Kurukshetra" that "while the tail and hair growth have been shed, beastliness is yet to be shed".

It is also true that at any given point of time, divinity manifests itself to a higher degree in certain people. It is the imperative duty of educator to help advance and accelerate this manifestation of divinity or in Vivekananda's words 'the development and expression of the perfection inherent in every individual.'

Education today unfortunately focuses only on narrow cognitive aspect of one's personality. Even in this, we find that the schools are increasingly unable to handle the aggressive, greedy, dishonest and angry people, whether they are parents or children. If we want value oriented education, we must strengthen school's capability to create a climate in which children can imbibe values and consider them important for their own benefit and for the benefit of humanity.

Such an approach of creating a climate of values in the school may be termed as "Managerial approach to value education". By whatever name we may call it, it will be a necessary and significant new direction. The creation of such a value-oriented climate is necessary, particularly in the modern context when the traditional "disciplinary climate" in schools has broken down or is under severe strain. If schools develop higher competent and efficient persons in terms of skills and in terms of providing goods in the market and fail to foster self-discipline among the students, they cannot contribute either to the individual's happiness or to social good.

Contribution of Bharatiya Vidya Bhavan

Bharatiya Vidya Bhavan was founded by Dr. K.M. Munshi, a decade before the dawn of India's independence. It has steadily grown into a comprehensive, co-operative national movement, with an International outlook, for the promotion of ethical and spiritual values. It has today 110 institutions in the country—several schools and colleges and many job-oriented courses. It has also centres abroad to propagate Indian culture. In Kulapati Munshi's words: "It stands for the age-old but ever young *Vedic* concepts of *Rita*, *Satya*, *Yajna* and *Tapas* which, in modern parlance, mean the supremacy of the Majesty of the Moral Law anchored in *Dharma*; complete accord of thought, word and dead, which is *Satya*; discipline or self control by obliterating selfishness, erasing the ego, which is *Samyama*; and acting with a sense of dedication of God— an attitude of *Ishvara Pranidhana*—which is *Samarapana*. *Dharma* by itself encapsulates—*Satyam, Shivam, Sundaram*—the Grecian ideals of Truth, Goodness and Beauty.

Bharatiya Vidya Bhavan had the blessings of national leaders like Gandhiji, Jawaharlal Nehru, Sardar Patel, Dr. Rajendra Prasad and Shri C. Rajagopalachari. It subscribes to Gandhiji's views that Science, without spiritual values, would result in *Sarvanash*—total ruination, and science with spiritual values would lead to *Sarvodaya*—total welfare of all. It believes with Shri C. Rajagopalachari: "Information has to be transformed and made to blossom into knowledge and, knowledge should mature into wisdom. Otherwise, it would be a useless tinsel".

Bhavan believes in reshaping and ushering in world without borders in accordance with India's age-old ideal of "Vasudhaiva Kutumbakam". Recently Bharatiya Vidya Bhavan, New York organised a unique event on September 21, 2002. On this occasion, particular attention was drawn to Swami Vivekananda's historic address at the 'World's Parliament of Religions' in 1893, particularly on the opening day of September 11, 1893. It was another September 11, quite different from 11 September, 2001 which is also in some sense, a consequence of the failure to respond to the clarion call given by Swami Vivekananda on September 11, 1893. On that day in Chicago, Swami Vivekananda drew attention to the truth, wonderful doctrine preached in the Gita.

"Whosoever comes to Me, through whatsoever form, I reach him; all men are struggling through paths which in the end lead to Me. A nobler statement of inter-faith movement we cannot easily find". Further, in his speech, Swami Vivekananda said,

"Sectarianism, bigotry, and its horrible descendant, fanaticism, have long possessed this beautiful earth. They have filled the earth with violence, drenched it often and often with human blood, destroyed civilisation and sent whole nations to despair".

Swami Vivekananda further hoped that the "bell that tolled this morning in honour of this convention may be the death-knell of all fanaticism, of all persecutions with the sword or with the pen, and of all uncharitable feelings between persons wending their way to the same goal".

Conclusion

But during the year between 1893 and 2001, fanaticism and intolerance did not come down, rather they have increased and caused great harm to man kind.

Education in the 21st century has, therefore, a very special challenge of promoting inter-faith harmony, tolerance and understanding and in promoting spiritual and moral values to complement the great scientific and technological advances in the material sphere.

School Curriculum for Global Peace

JIVA Experience

Steven Paul Rudolph

Now more than ever is a time for us to take action for providing novel educational methods that promote world peace. Far too much has been said, and way too little has been done practically to provide students and teachers with tangible experiences that promote global peace and harmony. The antiquated syllabi followed by most schools and the limited benefit afforded by talk-and-chalk methodologies must give way to a new type of education that is less instructive and more constructive in its orientation.

The very nature of learning itself is construction. It is not merely a process of listening and memorizing—for such "learning" cannot be considered learning at all. It is no different than pumping plants full of steroids to make them artificially grow. And what can one expect from such plants bred of unnatural chemicals, fruits that are poisonous and which only lead to contaminating the bodies and minds of those who eat. The actions of those who eat contaminated food may themselves be contaminated and lead to undesirable ends.

Students today imbibe so much information to pass their exams and resort to cheating and unfair means to get the highest marks possible—all at the expense of learning what it means to be human. Is it any wonder why there is so much corruption and social unrest in our society? The education system today has actually become the basis for cheating, hatred, distrust and discord which seriously affects us on a day-to-day basis. Let us not be so blind as the smoker who suffers from lung cancer, but continues to smoke.

A peaceful person is one who is realised. And this realisation comes about through learning. Learning occurs through a building process, where each individual constructs his or her unique understanding of the world based upon information—input in connection with one's environment and experiences. If provided with the proper environment and experiences (as expert gardeners provide to their plants), learners will maximise their full potential towards becoming rational, pious, and peace-loving individuals.

But how to go about providing a peace-enhanced curriculum? We have to answer the question of the going last mile, where all our eloquent words are converted into hardcore, tangible artifacts for students and teachers. We have to ask the hard questions such as: Whose job is it to undertake this work? The Social Studies teacher's? The English teacher's? Where does it fit into the curriculum as a whole? Who is responsible for enhancing the curriculum? The school? The NCERT?

Jiva Institute is a non-profit research and development organisation founded in 1992 which is working to create a healthy, wealthy, and fearless society. As per NCERT's National Curriculum Framework (2001), the NCERT has called on such non-government organisations (NGOs) to come forward with solutions to the educational dilemma that India faces today.

Jiva has tackled this challenge in three ways:

1) Enhancing the existing NCERT Curriculum,

2) Creating teaching and learning materials and methodologies for teaching value and peace-based curriculum, and

3) Developing a teacher training program that helps teachers and school administrators create environments conducive to value and peace-based learning.

Enhancing the Syllabus

Our first step was to create an enhanced curriculum, based on the NCERT Curriculum Framework Guidelines that incorporated elements of a peace-based syllabus. (We have labeled this new curriculum as ICOT—India's Curriculum of Tomorrow.) This was done through a detailed process of creating educational standards (statements that students should be able to know and do) for each year. These standards were then organised across the curriculum for all subjects. In other words, the concepts of values and peace were not just allocated to a subject like Moral Science or Social Studies, but rather, were thematically integrated with all subjects, including Mathematics, Science, Languages, and even Art. As adults, humane and peaceful dealings are not behaviors that we limit to a portion of our day (hopefully)—they pervade our entire lives. As such, these topics must not be relegated to small portion of the syllabus, but must pervade the syllabus in its entirety.

Creating Materials and Methodologies

Our second step was to create a new set of learning materials and methodologies that teachers could use in their classrooms to produce the right kind of environments—ones that encourage teamwork, respect, and so on. The textbooks we created deal extensively with a vast array of values in all subjects. For example, in computers, children learn how technology can also be used destructively, and are asked to consider the responsibility inventors have in creating new technologies. In Science, students learn not only about where clean water comes from, but how people are affected by the lack of it, and what they can do to help their fellow country-people in attaining their basic needs. In Maths and Geography, students learn about statistics of human rights abuse in India and throughout the world.

Jiva has also introduced a methodology of teaching called "cooperative learning", a means of having students spend much of their classtime interacting in groups rather than sitting in rows listening to the teacher's lecture. Students gain tremendously from this practice because not only does it provide them with a greater exposure to the content, but it also helps them gain badly needed social skills such as discussion, debate, conflict-resolution, turn-taking, teamwork and so on. Students become better disciplined and more responsible while working in their groups, as their responsibility extends beyond the mere individual scoring on exams. They now have a duty to perform well for the benefit of their peers, too.

Value and Peace-Based Teacher Training

Our third step was to create a teacher-training program that teaches teachers how to teach values and peace in all subjects. This training program is available now through seminar format, and has already been successfully run under a program conducted and organised by the NCERT in July 2001. Teachers learn how to incorporate the topics of values and peace into their subject no matter which subject it may be. They learn how to create a constructive-based lesson plans, using resources available to them locally, how to localise it for their specific purposes, how to review and critique these lessons, and how to make them available on the Internet for other teachers to access and use. The course will shortly be available via the Internet through an e-learning course.

Conclusion

In short, Jiva has taken definitive steps toward inculcating values and peace among the students and teachers of India through a three-pronged approach: curriculum enhancement, creation of materials and methodologies, and the development of a teacher-training program. This work, under the banner of ICOT, is based on the principle of constructive education, which facilitates the creation of environments that are conducive to realised learning.

The corollary to Jiva's approach with ICOT of constructive learning as an instructive practice is social constructivism, or rather, a general sentiment that leads toward the positive development of the society. In other words, learners who undergo an education in constructive learning environments will naturally and automatically extend their minds and energy in positive ways into their society. This might be in the form of art, journalism, environmental practices, driving practices, architecture, social help, uncorrupt political practices, and so on.

Therefore if we hope to see a more civil and peaceful society and world, we must start at a local level. Erudite lectures may provide a sense of light, however, not even the most common of common people need to be convinced that honesty is superior to dishonesty, that justice surpasses injustice, that values stand above corruption, and that peace is preferable to war. What we need are practical models in action that go the last mile—that transform the wisdom and scholarly vision espoused by great social and spiritual leaders into real materials that students and teachers can use immediately. Through ICOT, Jiva has made a humble step in achieving this vision, so that our generation, and the ones after, might live in a world that is more peaceful than the one we live in today.

Value Orientation of Teachers

Bodhpriya Jaibharti

Value orientation of teacher education is our supreme need today. Tagore said, "The highest education is that which does not merely give us information but makes our life in harmony with all existences". While emphasizing the role of teacher in the society, Dr KM Munshi said, "The teacher is the principal driving force in a dynamic society, and his (her) leadership is most important, if not essential to free India, which is being built up anew from the bottoms upward. It is very wisely said, a nation is as great as its schools and its schools are as great as its teachers. Only good students can become great teachers Therefore, it is necessary that we apply our minds to the oldest convocation address which is included in the *Taittiriya Upanishad*.

"Speak the truth. Walk in the way of the duty, neglect not the study of knowledge, treat the teachers with respect and gratitude, and fail not in taking upon thyself the burden of life, neglect not truth, nor thy duty, nor social welfare nor thy own good, nor the study and teaching of higher knowledge, neglect not thy duties unto God, treat men of high learning and character with respect, give them what you can with faith and reverence, in thy actions behave as do such men of high character and learning, Even as they do, do thou likewise."

This is the teaching, this is the exhortation, this is the doctrine of high knowledge. Thus, the education system consisting of educational institutions, teachers and students must own up the responsibility of building a resurgent India in a global society, on the basis of moral, social and spiritual values on the one hand and physical, aesthetic and economic values on the other hand.

Values and Education

Values refer to objects, experiences, achievements that we consider desirable and valuable for our existence and evolution; for moksha from evil and suffering, and evolution into *joy* and evolution of our inner and outer environment. Education, especially value education, is the process of bringing about desirable change of behavior. Various goals of value education are creativity, commitment to human values, social justice, national cohesion, and scientific temper, independence of mind and spirit, secularism, socialism and democracy. To realise this aim, we design curriculum.

Need for Value Education

All good education is a process of developing the human personality—intellectual, physical, social, moral, aesthetic and spiritual. But education, today, has degenerated into a process of information—transformation with the sole objective of passing examination. Lot of anti-values are developing very fast in our total life. Anti-values like—deculturisation, dehumanisation, social alienation, casteism, social and national disintegration have become active.

The population increase has seriously affected the quality of life of the masses. Crime, corruption, violence and indifference to human suffering have spread to all walks of life. Our physical environment is growing increasingly polluted and depleted. Narrow communalism, casteism, linguist and regional outlook are dividing our people and coming in the way of our developing a unifying national and global outlook. The world today faces a catastrophe, threatened with nuclear holocaust. As never before in the history of mankind, we are in need of peace and understanding. Therefore we need a value education crusade, laying code of conduct in society, code for all 5 relationships - physical, botanical, animal, human and divine.

Scope of Value Education

What is the scope of value education in school education?

Firstly, value education involves all the faculties of our personality—knowing, feeling and willing. The child should be made aware of the right values, to feel the proper emotions, and internalise values in thought, word and deed.

Secondly, certain values have to be developed as habits in the child, *e.g.* cleanliness, punctuality, regularity and so on. Value education should be related to the child's psychological readiness and experiences.

Thirdly, at the early stage, value education should be provided through concrete activity and live situations. At the later stages, the students should develop a rational understanding of the values and internalise them in thought, feeling and action. All values we have mentioned earlier are relevant to all the stages, but activities are different.

What Values Should be Fostered?

Man or woman exists not as a solitary individual living in a vacuum, but as an active member of a dynamic, social group, society, national and global community. The value education of a person should be related to the specific socio-cultural context in which he lives, and with reference to some universal and eternal values.

What are our social and national concerns today and what demands they make on our value education? The National Policy on Education, 1986 (NPE-86) says, "In our plural society, education should foster universal and eternal values, oriented towards unity and integration of our people. Such value education should help eliminate "obscurantism, religious fanaticism, violence, superstition and fatalism". Universal values given in our constitution are liberty, equality, fraternity, democracy, socialism and secularism." The core elements are:

1. Common cultural heritage
2. Equalitarianism, Democracy, Socialism & Secularism
3. Equality of Sexes
4. Protection of the environment
5. Removal of social barriers

6. Observance of the small family norm
7. Scientific temper and Humanism
8. Pursuit of human excellence

The Process of Value Education

The process consists of 5 steps:

1. Development of Value Consciousness

It is a complex network of environmental factors, home influences, peer group, community, the mass media and the society at large. It involves developing a sensitivity to values, ability to choose the right values in accordance with one's conception of the highest ideal of life i.e. Truth, Goodness and Beauty, internalising them, realising them in one's life. It is a life long quest.

2. Development of Value Clarification

The world of values is as vast as the world of facts. Each fact has corresponding value. Fact and values are two sides of the same coin. Therefore, world of values is very complicated. We need to rationally analyse each value and identify corresponding emotion, which will give clarity to each value.

3. Development of Value Judgements

Life is a series of challenges, each challenge calls for a judgement as to what to do or not to do. We need the mind of a judge to apply the whole law to a particular case. The development of this faculty is most difficult in the whole process of value development.

4. Development of Value Motivation

Having developed consciousness, clarification and judgment, one feels motivated to live values. It needs moral courage. There are numerous methods of developing moral courage as a motivator, along with moral indignation. The best method is to live with persons who are highly motivated to live values through all the human faculties such as knowing, feeling and willing. When we develop strong will in favor of values, value action flows from our being.

5. Value Oriented Action

Value oriented action is supreme *Dharma*, It is the *summum bonum* of life This is the gist of the teaching of Bhagwan Krishna, of all the spiritual personalities and secular philosophers of values like Socrates. Dev Atma has done excellent work in this field..

Sources of Value Education

There are several sources and the teachers have to make use of them judiciously. Firstly, the regular subject areas are reservoir of values. Science is conducive to free inquiry, commitment to truth, scientific method and scientific temper. Mathematics promotes logical thinking, neatness and precision. All subjects promote specific values. Secondly, co-curricular activities are very effective in inculcating values in children. The students, self-government in schools, various hobby clubs and associations, NCC, NSS, Scouting & girl Guides, Red Cross, excursions and field visits, sports and games promote pursuit of common goals and values. Children develop creativity, distinctive intellectual, social and cultural interests, the values of democratic living, responsibility, cooperation, tolerance and secularism. Thus values are imbibed by living. Tagore and Gandhi laid great stress on the creation of a conducive atmosphere in educational institutions for the wholesome development of the personality of the child. The school influences through environment generated by it, its setting, its traditions, its ideas etc. Its teachers work with dedication, mutual respect, affection and love. Parents, students, community, teachers and management are united by work for value development.

Value educators have set fine examples for us to research and learn. They developed values in students by their own example and years of hard work. Sri Sathya Sai Baba has developed education for human values at *Puttaparthi*.

Strategies and Methods for Developing Values

Value education can be provided directly, indirectly and incidentally. Direct value education refers to deliberate systematic instruction in values. The values to be inculcated are explained, discussed, and illustrated through stories and real life events. This instruction is given as per prescribed value education syllabus and during the allotted period. Indirectly, value education can be imparted through regular subjects of the school curriculum and co-curricular activities. Value education is incidental when some specific event is observed and discussed *e.g.* acts of bravery. The event may be one to be emulated or disparaged. There are many more methods of developing values in students. Some of these are:

1. Influencing by own personality.
2. Lecture, discussion and question answer sessions.
3. Self-examination.
4. Associating with saints and other noble persons.
5. Community service.
6. Service of animals.
7. Tending plants.
8. Donating money for reducing suffering.
9. Role-play of heroes of India and other nations.
10. Poetry, music, dance, drama, especially group singing.
11. Reading books on values.
12. Joining organisations like Red Cross, Social Hygiene Association, Blood Bank, Eye Bank, World Association for Value Education.
13. Participating in national, cultural, ethical functions.
14. Making and following up monthly chart of value development exercises and activities.
15. Sports, games, athletics, martial arts.
16. Scouting, NCC, NSS, Hiking, Rock climbing, excursions.
17. Seminars, summer camps.
18. Helping victims of natural and other calamities.
19. Service of parents, teachers and all other benefactors.
20. Providing services in social gatherings in School, Church, Mosque, *Gurudwara*, Budh Vihar and other places.
21. In time of war, caring for injured soldiers.

22. Social adoption of children from weaker sections (orphans), serving old persons.

23. Prayer to the Divine in Nature.

24. Study about the ideas and deeds of great human beings and follow their example.

25. Keep a diary of our good and bad desires and deeds. It helps us in self–analysis. "Know thyself," said Lord Buddha.

26. Repeatedly, wish others well. This is called Shubh Kamana.

27. When watching movies, judging whether the words, ideas and deeds are good or bad. This will develop hatred for evil and love for good.

28. Avoid the company of those who have bad habits, those who are frivolous.

29. Seek company of the wise, diligent, altruistic, development minded people.

Teacher's Role

Our role as teachers is:

1. Help to create an atmosphere of love, trust and security in the school.

2. Understand the child and its developmental characteristics.

3. Relate value education to concrete situations. Do not preach.

4. Organise value education indirectly. Let children learn through living. Co-curricular activities are effective.

5. Use deliberate, direct, value education continuously.

6. Help the students to understand the subject in its totality, information, content, logical structure, method and qualities of mind and disposition it is associated with.

7. Teachers influence students with their total personality. Let them therefore develop their own personality.

8. Example is better than precept. If we love our subject, our students are likely to love it too. If we are concerned about the environment of the school, if we are punctual, responsible, our students are likely to follow our example.

Mere emulation is not education. We want children not to do things in blind faith, custom or tradition, but after rational deliberation and thought.

Friends, having got fairly good idea of our value education crusade for building the whole character of our nation as also of total humanity; let us get on to the mission of National Global Development through building higher character of all our citizens.

Conclusion

Value Education is necessary to build character; it is the value that make a human living different from other being. It is only through such holistic education in knowledge and value, as professed by Mahatma Gandhi, it will be possible to create global citizens.

Role modeling is the most effective means of value education. Teachers are, rightly or wrongly, the role models for students. Hence value education of teachers is a necessary prerequisite of value development in students.

Inter-faith and Education in DAV School

G.P. Chopra

There is a definite need to discuss, debate and design strategies to meet the challenges of the 21st Century in which the whole world has become a global society because of technology. Technology has brought us enormous benefits—ships and railroads, telegraphs and telephones, the autos and aeroplanes, electricity, television and the computer. Distances have disappeared and barriers have vanished. Satellites are being used for making long distance calls to the remotest parts of the world. There is a growing dependence on videophones, microphones, cellular mobile phones, Cable TV, Pagers, E-mail, Microchips, Microwaves, Robots, etc. Because of the advancement of science, many miracles are being performed. Many dreaded diseases have been eradicated.

Eminent and respectable scientists are talking about possibilities that stagger the imagination. Should we breed people with cow like stomach so that they can digest grass thereby solving the food problem? Should we attempt to eliminate inferior people and breed a super race? Hitler tried this but he did not have the genetic weapons in his laboratories. Should we clone soldiers to do our fighting? Should we have reserve organs for ourselves—each of us having a "savings bank" full of livers, lungs, etc.

Thus man has all the reasons to be happy on his victory over the forces of nature and yet as Hardy said in one of his novels, "in many parts of the world, for many people happiness is but an occasional episode in a general drama of pain". And sadly, the greatest threat to man's happiness and well being is posed by man himself and that too in the name of faith, in the name of religion. Every age in the history of human civilisation has witnessed the worst kind of atrocities and excesses perpetrated in the name of religion by people who swore by their faith and killed by their swords. Their's was the faith that erected barriers and built walls, spread hatred and dealt death. And sadly again, there is a world of difference between what people preach and what they practise because no religion preaches hatred or violence.

Inter-faith

All the religions of the world teach us that we should be kind and considerate to our fellowmen because all men are created equal. The Atharva Veda says: "Like heartedness, like mindedness, non-hostility do I create for you. Do show affection one to the other, as does the cow to her new born. As the mother protects her only son even at the risk of her own life, so one should enlarge one's heart infinitely with compassion for all beings." This doctrine in the Vedas is reflected in the teachings of the Christian and the Jewish religions, "Do not do unto others what is hateful to you. God will know it. Do unto others as you would have them do unto you". The beliefs of the Buddhists, and the Confucians and the Muslims are the same and reflect similar attitudes with regard to man's relation to man. In Holy *Quran* also there is an injunction that all men belong to the same fraternity and should be treated with the same dignity and respect as the Muslims. There is also a condition laid down that before anyone can be condemned, he shall have the right to be heard in his own defence.

However, in the 20th Century we have seen new forms and scales of violence and so much hatred and bloodshed in the name of religion. Unity in diversity is the plan of the creator and this plan we need to imbibe and disseminate through education. To impose a single faith on others through coercion, to convert people to your professed faith through allurements is a sin. Lord Krishna has clearly declared in the Gita, "I am in every religion as a thread through a string of pearls. Whenever thou seest extraordinary holiness and extraordinary power, raising and purifying humanity, know that I am there." For education to fight all evils, it has to be reinforced by the religion of tolerance, acceptance, love and harmony. And this can be achieved only by exposure to and understanding all other faiths.

Inter-faith Education in DAV Schools

In all of our DAV schools spread across the country, the students are taught to have respect for all the religions and there are no distinctions of caste and creed. In some of our schools in Bihar, for example, the number of Muslim students is more or less the same as the number of Hindu students. We have nearly 30 per cent Sikh students in our schools and colleges in Punjab, and even when militancy in Punjab was at its highest, peace and calm prevailed in our institutions. In the disturbed North East, the Christians, the Hindus and the students of other faiths in our schools live in peace and harmony.

This is because in our schools to give moral and religious education to the students has always been a fundamental function. In addition to this, for the past several years, we have been holding "Charitra Nirman Shiviras" at regular intervals in our schools. These Shiviras have become a mass movement and acclamation received from the parents and the students about these shiviras is highly significant. I am sure that lakhs of students coming out of DAV schools and colleges will definitely make a big difference in the tone of the country.

From class V onwards, we have Dharam Shiksha books prescribed for all the students in our schools. At the end of the year an examination is held. It is gratifying to note that the number of students who opt to sit for the examination is gradually going up. Last year, about 35,000 students sat for the examination. The students who do exceptionally well are invited to Delhi and are awarded prizes. We have a number of schools in Nepal, Mauritius and some other countries, where students of all faith study in peace and amity.

However, in many places Religion as an academic exercise has all but disappeared. As a result, there is a disturbing increase in the incidence of abnormal behaviour among students all over the world—indiscipline, drug addiction, defiance of authority etc.

These students seem to be adrift and they are bringing a bad name to themselves and to the institution in which they studied. However where religious instruction is given, students are less likely to be afflicted by this malady. It is suggested that religious and moral education should be a part of the curriculum globally for the global society because it will teach the students to respect all religions and to be good and responsible citizens.

Concern for Environment

The degradation of environment is one of the most serious challenges facing the world in the 21st Century. The deforestation poses a great threat not only to the ecosystem but also to our very survival on this planet. During the last 50 years, half of the world's forests have vanished. Six million hectares of earth's surface are turning into desert every year. We are losing 32,700 million tons of top fertile soil annually. This is a matter of utmost worry because soil formation is a very slow process and soil loss is an irreversible disaster. Deforestation disregards the needs of wild life, and hundreds of birds and animals have become extinct. Every bird and animal has a purpose in the ecological chain. When a species disappears, the delicate chain is broken. We have to work not only for man's security but for his happiness also. And the unique abilities of some of these creatures makes us wonder. For example, there are bats with sonar which can avoid any obstruction by bouncing high frequency sound from it. If there are bugs in trees, a living tool will get them out—the drill of the wood pecker. And when small animals die, there is that specialist—the beetle that buries them. As master pieces of art bring joy and wonder, so does wild life. A leopard, a gazelle, a dolphin are as much a priceless part of our human heritage as a great temple or a symphony by a great music master. Unless trees are planted on a massive scale globally, man's existence on this planet will be in peril.

The forests have been a stronghold of spirituality for millions of people regardless of their religious beliefs. There is music in the whispering of the trees when the breeze blows. The gospel of

Nature speaks its parables from the forest covered with flowers. In the silence of the forest is hidden the source of His love. The eye of faith alone can unveil and see the illumination of that love. When a man sits in the forest in the morning and in the evening he can see this beauty all around and this beauty is an inseparable aspect of the Lord. Because of its beautiful forests, Kipling once said that India is a place fit for gods, not for ordinary human beings.

Some months back I wrote a letter to all the Principals of DAV Schools and Colleges across the country, asking them to plant trees in large numbers on their campuses in order to prevent further degradation of our environment. I am glad to say that the response has been magnificent in that thousands and thousands of trees have been planted and are being taken care of. It has been demonstrated around the world that the youth have a fire power and if the project of planting trees can be taken up by them globally, it will be a remarkable contribution in saving our planet.

Women

Another topic requiring our attention is woman's place in society. Hindus regard woman as a goddess and it is said that where women are worshipped, gods dwell. Some faiths say that while man was fashioned out of the dust of the earth, woman was created in god's own image. History tells of women whose names have been written in letters of gold in all countries of the world. However, women today in most parts of the world are leading miserable lives. They are discriminated on the basis of sex. They are exploited as wage earners. They earn only one third or half salary of their male counterparts. Since the upper jobs are reserved for men they get only low paid jobs. They are employed as domestic help or as cheap labour for construction work. Employed women continue to bear the burden of domestic work and child care. They are humiliated at home and in the office and they feel lonely and frustrated. Man's inhumanity to women is writ large in scarlet letters on the pages of history. Innocent women who are unwary of the ways of man are trapped and a poet pleads with the world to be kinder to them.

O World be nobler for her sake
If she but knew thee what thou art,
What wrongs are borne, what deeds are done,
In thee, beneath thy daily sun,
Her heart for pain and shame would break
O world be noble for her sake.

Since women form 50% of the world population, the world can progress only if women are treated as equal partners. Let us bring in winds of change and let us not forget our debt to womankind.

In the dark womb where we began
Our mother's life made us a man
Through all the months of human birth
Their beauty fed our common earth
We could not see, nor breathe nor stir
But through the death of some of her.

What have we done to keep in mind
Our debt to all the womankind?
What woman's happier life repays
For all those months of wretched days?
For all our mouthless body leeched,
Ere birth's releasing hell was reached?

What have we done or tried or said
In thanks to women alive or dead
Men triumph over women still,
Men trample women's rights at will,
And man's lust roves the world untamed.

There can be few things more worthwhile today than improving the lot of women—on it will dependent the kind of world we will have in which our grand children will survive. There has to be an incessant war globally for the emancipation of women through lectures and debates, publications of books and pamphlets, founding of more schools and colleges for women.

In our institutions we give special attention to the education of girls and during the last decade their enrolment has gone up tremendously. Education is a proper career for girls and we have several colleges of education, some exclusively for girls. There are other institutions where we prepare them for entry into medical and engineering colleges and also for entry into other professions and we have courses like Home Science which are useful to them. And many of our girls are landing with very good jobs. In our own Institutions, women are being employed in large numbers. To give just one example, in our schools in Delhi or near about as against 2500 women teachers, there are only about 200 male members of the staff.

Population

Another area of great concern is the tremendous Population Explosion all over the world. It took the world 1600 years to double its population, which has now been doubled in 33 years and is going to double again in 30 years. It is this tremendous increase in population which is eating into the vitals of world economy. Inspite of all the propaganda against large families, the baby boom continues particularly in the countries of the third world. However, a desirable decision in favour of small family can be taken only by those who are literate. But a vast majority of the people in these countries are illiterate and the vicious circle continues.

India's growing population is a big challenge for the environment, health and hygiene, housing and nutrition. The increasing numbers in India threaten natural resources including land, water and environment. Finding employment for all those who come out of Colleges and Universities is going to be a big problem. The Central Board of Secondary Education in co-operation with Ministry of Human Resource Development, and United Nations Population Fund has started a project called population and development. Under this project teachers will be trained to make the students aware of the dangers of over population. The CBSE has sought support from DAV College Managing Committee for the successful implementation of the project. Approximately 140 DAV Public Schools will be covered under the project in some of the states at the initial stage.

If progress is to be made towards family planning, the colleges and universities everywhere will have to join hands and make people aware of the dangers of population explosion. The problem of growing population is being compounded by some faiths which forbid abortion.

Human Rights

We need to consider the problem of human rights. This problem affects humanity at large; and although all nations affirm that these rights should be protected; yet in actual practice these rights are being progressively eroded and man's inhumanity to man persists. Women and children suffer the most. Children who should go to school are made to work like slaves in factories and women are sexually harassed in their places of work. Many people in many parts of the world, particularly in the third world are uneducated, without pleasure or hope, tired, plundered or cheated. That is why the Bard said, "It grieves my heart to consider, what man has made of man". The prophets of Israel used to say:

"O Lord of the universe, will thou cause thine ear to hear the fatherless and the oppressed so that the man of the earth, may no longer oppress".

But it is these disadvantaged and downtrodden sections of society on whose labour the world lives. This compels us to ask ourselves whether a form of society, which depends on the toil of these persons robs them even of their livelihood is right. They have borne the main burden of history without complaining and without reward:

> *"The emptiness of ages in their face*
> *And on their back the burden of the world*
> *Is this the thing the Lord God made and gave*
> *To have dominion on our sea and land?"*

> *There is no shape more terrible than theirs*
> *More tongued with censure of the world's blind greed*
> *More packed with danger to the universe.*
> *O masters, Lords and rulers in all lands*

How will it be with kingdoms and with kings
With those who shaped them to the things they are
When this dumb terror shall rise to judge the world
After the silence of the centuries.

On our part we are doing what we can to better the lot of some such segments of society. Swami Dayanand, the founder of the Arya Samaj, was one of the greatest reformers of the 19th Century. All his life, he tried to bring cheer into the lives of the out-castes and the downtrodden sections of society. That is why he laid stress in opening of schools and colleges so that through education their lives could improve. Gandhiji once said that even if Swami Dayanand had done nothing other than what he did for improving a lot of these men, women and children, his name would have been immortal.

Following the footsteps of Swami Dayanand many of our schools have taken certain steps to arrange for the education of the slum dwelling children. They are being given totally free education and lakhs of rupees are being spent on them. Women from slums are taught tailoring, sewing, embroidery and the three Rs' and they are also taught how to operate the bank accounts so that they can stand on their own feet. There are a number of orphanages for children and a few schools where mentally retarded children are taken care of.

Conclusion

It is admitted` that the world on the whole will benefit from Globalisation but I want to sound a note of warning about one or two things. With the globe's diminishing resources and expanding population, the benefits of technology are irresistible but its dangers remain unknown and perhaps one day ungovernable. We should remember that technology once let loose is not easily controlled. With the cell and the atom, man toys with the basic building blocks of the universe and perhaps with his own extinction. For if there is nothing noble about man's curiosity, there is also something quite profane. The threats posed by technology—whether of chemical pollution, of nuclear power or of electronic surveillance—boldly need to be debated and more and more widely understood in our colleges and universities. While in the years ahead, there will be more and more pressure on us to have more and more technology, we would ignore liberal education at our own peril. Reading Shakespeare or Homer or Kalidas is one of life's deepest pleasures and education that permits access to these and similar delight should not be ignored. It excites the brain's circuits and causes them to glow.

The sweep of TV is global and T.V. is also creating a big problem, an electronic culture, often at the expense of written tradition around which education was once constructed. Students spend so many hours a week before television that no one understands just how many hundreds of hours before the TV sets may be altering the way in which our minds perform and the culture they contain.

Globalisation may also have a detrimental effect on the sovereignty of states. There are huge disparities between the income and wealth of nations and therefore a single world economy will be difficult. There also may be a clash of cultures.

We are one sixth of the total population of the world and a very important part of the globe. What we do here with respect to religious harmony, the lot of women, population explosion, human rights, etc. will have a great impact on the rest of the world. And, in India, saints and sages of all faiths have been teaching the value of love and affection, contentment and honesty that have enabled us to survive for thousands of years.

It is true that across the globe now the weather is cold and grey but the fog will begin to disappear if colleges and the universities all over the world can give a message to the people that hymns of the Vedas are prayer for peace on earth and good will among all faiths.

Role of Universities in Fostering a Harmonious Global Society

K. Mathews

The widespread intolerance leading to tragic conflicts particularly in the post-cold-war years prompted UNESCO to revive the quest for tolerance, and acting on this initiative, the UN General Assembly proclaimed 1995 as the United Nations' Year of Tolerance. In that year UNESCO adopted a Declaration of Principles of Tolerance and a Plan of Action to follow up the year. In 1996, UN General Assembly invited Member States to observe the International Day of Tolerance on 16th November every year. Paradoxically, however, in the past six years, since the first observance of this 'International Day of Tolerance', the world community has witnessed an alarming rise of xenophobia, aggressive nationalism, chauvinism, religious fundamentalism and international terrorism. Since tolerance is one of the most important conditions for the achievement of the culture of peace, the year 2000, the Millennium Year, was declared and observed as the International Year for the Culture of Peace. This brought the issue of tolerance into even sharper focus. With the religious summit in New York in August 2000, greater emphasis was placed on the need for removal of religious intolerance.

Intolerance is most often based on fear and rejection of the unknown, on prejudices based on the lack of knowledge about the "other" or on deliberate propaganda designed to present "the other" in the most unfavourable light, mostly for political purposes. In all cases the remedy is to educate, inform and empower individuals to assume the responsibilities of dialogue, mutual respect and tolerance. Further more, last year, 2001, was the United

Nations' Year of Dialogue among Civilisations, with the noble goal to nurture the dialogue, which removes the perception of diversity as a threat and helps prevent conflicts, underlining tolerance and respect for diversity.

But as far as the global efforts were concerned, the year, 2001, highlighted the need for tolerance with unprecedented clarity and urgency. A terrible threshold was crossed in September 2001, in the escalation of intolerance, violence and terrorism. The terrorist outrages of 11 September in New York and Washington and 13 December (2001) in New Delhi are, apart from attacks on America and India, offences against human dignity, crimes against humanity and the essential purposes of the United Nations system and civilised existence. This blind, criminal violence has been perpetrated in the midst of the United Nations Year of Dialogue among Civilisations, itself following on from the International Year of Culture of Peace!! Are we to conclude therefore that international efforts to promote an ideal of tolerance and peace, mutual understanding and solidarity are in vain and that these goals are unattainable? Far from it.

The Need

It is all the more reason to step up action to eradicate the deep-seated causes of violence. These include poverty and exclusion, ignorance and discrimination. There is an ever-greater need today to work in close partnership to develop an overall strategy encompassing the social, economic, and cultural dimensions. This unwavering solidarity of thought and action is essential to counter injustice and dangers of a certain form of globalisation, thereby eliminating intolerance and fanaticism. There is a need to rethink globalisation and give it a more human, more equitable face, espousing values other than those of the market place. The General Conference of the UNESCO, at its 31st session that ended on the 2nd November 2001 has adopted unanimously the first Universal Declaration on Cultural Diversity. The recognition of all our creative diversity is a crucial step that affirms our adherence to common ethical values and principles. Prompted equally by the respect for human rights and fundamental freedoms and openness towards others—recognised as both different from and similar to ourselves—tolerance is the very foundation of dialogue and pluralism. Today more than ever before it needs to be put into practice, particularly through education at all levels. It is not only a requirement of the Year of Dialogue among Civilisations (2001), but also a condition for the application of the programme of Action of the World Conference against Racism, Racial Discrimination, Xenophobia and Related Intolerance, held in Durban, South Africa, in early September 2001, which has constituted a landmark in the struggle against racism and intolerance.

Some of the worst forms of intolerance find expression in racism, racial discrimination and xenophobia. The Durban Conference was aimed at drawing the world's attention to the issues and problems in this regard. The year 2001 has also been the International year of Mobilisation against Racism, Racial Discrimination, Xenophobia and Related Intolerance, aimed at attracting world's attention to the lofty objectives of the Durban Conference on racism, where the issue of tolerance, or the absence of it, was central in the discussions. No academic exercise on race, this UN Conference was instead an initiative to address the evils of intolerance and discrimination in whichever form or wherever they exist. It is not surprising therefore that the Durban Conference, provoked, among others, a debate on caste discrimination in India. Cast today enjoys unprecedented political leverage in India. The political establishment argued that since constitutional provisions for dealing with caste-based discriminations and disabilities are in place, caste is no longer a problem to be addressed. At the same time the protagonists of dalit identity have had considerable success, specially in recent years, in globalising their grievances. The United Nations, in the meanwhile, has become bolder in rejecting the erstwhile dogma that "internal matters" of nations should not be interfered with. Those who remain stuck with the mindset of nation states, though will take a while longer to get used to this hanging reality. Perhaps, the more we deny dignity and development to the *dalits* (untouchables) and try to keep this scandal under wraps, the surer we are to invite scrutiny and embarrassment in a fast globalising world.

It may also be noted that India was at the forefront of internationalising the opposition to apartheid. We should not be averse to debating caste objectively. For the race and caste are inhuman institutions and they deserve to be cast out, lock, stock and barrel. Race and caste leave indelible marks on their victims, physically and psychologically. Caste, like race is exploitative, discriminatory and anti-developmental. It is indeed, unfortunate that, even decades after Dr. B. R. Ambedkar issued the clarion call for its annihilation (see his book, Annihilation of Caste), caste continues to dominate the social, cultural and political horizon of India. Article 15 of the Indian Constitution outlaws discrimination on grounds of religion, race, caste, sex or place of birth. The fact that caste based discrimination has survived for so long in India and that it continues to prosper does not prove that it cannot be eradicated. Education has a crucial role in this area as well. It is unlikely that caste system will continue to remain immune to the challenge of the emerging global order, with the vulnerability of the nation-states implied in it. Caste is a blatant anachronism in a globalising world. The challenges of globalisation is a reality to be met.

Peace as a Mega-value

In a world full of hatred, chaos and contradictions, one is tempted to ask if the idea of peace and non-violence is just an illusion which will never be practiced, at least by megalomaniacs with obsession for power. In reference to the first war of this century following the horrendous terrorist attacks on America on September 11, it would be relevant to ask if peace can never be accepted as a mega-value or for that matter can man still hope to find inner harmony in the jungle of skirmishes and wars that our world has become. The word 'peace' describes a general social condition, where people are not agitated or discontented due to economic or other disparities. The term 'peace' also emerges here as a consequence of healthy relations among nations.

In India, Tirthankar Mahavir, the first metaphysical rebel, renounced the world only in protest against suffering and violence. Although an atheist, he emerged as a messiah of peace, and is today remembered for his philosophy of non-violence and many-sided approach to truth or Anekant. In his book, The Dynamics of Culture, Sorokin has mentioned that in the past 900 years most of the countries were involved in warfare 50 per cent of the time. Fighting, according to him, seems so natural with the human temperament that no amount of education can cure this universal malady. This is one view.

We are living in a society, which promotes utilitarian culture, where men are mere objects of utility. Men, though they refuse to be treated as things, are made to believe by politicians that war is indispensable. According to Griffith, "The art of politics is to persuade people that they make decisions while ensuring that they do not". Technology enhances this illusion further. Mass media has made every human situation so absurd and abstract that a civilian can never sense a real horror of war. Moreover, the production of arms in a highly industrialised society cannot be stopped for a hundred and one reasons especially because of a complex system of economy and international trade.

Power politics is the one greatest factor that mars the cause of peace. The decisions at all stage are taken on the basis of group thinking or group stupidity. Decisions, especially crucial ones are taken by a group of people. Its paradox is that the individual seldom suffers from a sense of guilt. As a team, group members suffer from the illusion of being true and sincere. How can one then cherish the idea of peace in the modern world? Now since faith has been replaced by reason, religion by politics, conscience by military strategy, personal courage by mechanical adventure and the individual by group-stupidity, it is better to fight against these and wage a war against the hell that is all around us. As the Constitution of UNESCO rightly noted, wars begin in the minds of men and therefore, the defences of peace should be constructed in the minds of men. It is here that special role of the Universities become clear.

The Role of Universities

As the Report of the World Conference on Higher Education 1998 has noted, it is no longer necessary to demonstrate the importance of education for sustainable, endogenous development, for democracy and for peace, for strengthening of the defence of peace as a human value and/or respect and protection of all human rights and fundamental freedoms. The far reaching changes now taking place in the world, and the entry of human values into a society based on knowledge and information, reveal how overwhelmingly important education and higher education are.

As Pandit Nehru rightly noted: "A University stands for humanism, for tolerance, for reason, for progress, for the adventure of ideas and for the search for truth. It stands for the onward march of the human race towards even higher objectives. If the Universities discharge their duty adequately, then it is well worth the nation and the people. But if the temple of learning itself becomes a home of narrow bigotry and petty objectives, how then will the nation prosper or a people grow in stature?". Humanism stresses the centrality of man. Tolerance is the basis for peace and development. As the UNESCO Declaration of Principles on Tolerance (1995) noted, tolerance is respect, acceptance and appreciation of the rich diversity of the world's cultures, our forms of expression and ways of being human. It is fostered by knowledge, openness, communication, and freedom of thought, conscience and belief. Tolerance is harmony in difference. It is not only a moral duty, it is also a political and legal requirement. Tolerance, the virtue that makes peace possible, contributes to the replacement of the culture of war by culture of peace (Art 1). Education is the most effective means of preventing intolerance. Education for tolerance, particularly at the University level should aim at countering influences that lead to fear and exclusion of others, and should help young people to develop capacities for independent judgement, critical thinking and ethical reasoning.

The University is one bulwark of peace. It is our universities and schools, which can and must build its stable defences. History teaches us that there is nothing automatic about peace. One cannot simply wish it and have it, or proclaim it and make it come true. Peace to be realised should be invented. The invention that peace calls for is the creation of conditions wherein international cooperation in all its forms and national action in all spheres in which we live our daily lives, will promote respect instead of indifference, tolerance instead of fear, understanding instead of misunderstanding and above all charity instead of hatred. Who can help create these positive conditions and banish the negative ones but university men and women, who are the inventive sector of human society everywhere.

Peace, if it is to be attained, must also be purchased. We are, after all, purchasing war at the price of unaccounted billions of dollars of our study, research and development in so far as we remain indifferent to the use of their results. We are paying for 'war preparedness, whatever they may mean.'

In this context there is an urgent and entirely practical call to our universities and educational systems in general to instill in the hearts and minds of their youth certain values and some insights. There is need for some sense of shame and feeling of regret for the technology brutalities of the present and the past suffered both by industrialised countries and imposed on the poor nations. The educational system should engender in its teachers and students a sense of social sympathy and compassion, a passionate sense of indignation against inequality and injustice. Knowledge, as 'Rig Veda' hymn celebrated in the very essence of morality, for those who forsake a companion in knowledge knows nothing of the part of right action. Given the national and international environment today, the Club of Rome's Report entitled: "The First Global Revolution" has aptly described our world as. "A small planet which we seem hell bent to destroy, bent with conflict, in an ideological and political vacuum, faced with problems of global dimensions which fading national states are impotent to solve, with immense scientific and technological possibilities for the improvement of the human condition, rich knowledge but poor in wisdom... Searching for the key to survival and sustainability".

Here I would like to emphasise the words "rich in knowledge and poor in wisdom" for they allude to the choices that will have to be made and the striving for wisdom that is so important. In this context it is pertinent to refer to T.S. Eliot, who in his *Choruses from the Rock*, has articulated the dilemma:

> *"Where is the Life we have lost in living?*
> *Where is the wisdom we have lost in knowledge?*
> *Where is the knowledge we have lost in information?"*

Many authoritative studies and reports produced by the United Nations and other experts have clearly shown that in the last two decades or so the disparities between rich and poor, haves and have-nots have not been reduced. They have in fact, increased. James Speth from the United Nations said, "If the present trends continue, economic disparities between industrial and developing nations will move from inequitable to inhuman" (Time, 29 July 1997, p. 13). It is no coincidence that these same two decades have also seen massive change in communication and technologies. Whatever technology has done for some of us, it has not uplifted the lives of most ordinary people. Nothing in our present experience suggests that this will change. Ordinary people see all these things and they may wonder what is that universities and those that learn there have occupied themselves with thus far. They may imagine that in the research laboratories, in the classrooms, in the quiet uncorrupted halls of academe, there are scholars who reflect on these issues, who encourage their students to reflect on these things, and will come out with some answers. Is their faith misplaced? It is quite clear that great issues of our time, issues involving survival and sustainability, issues about closing the gap between the haves and the have-nots, are going to require choices, choices about sharing, choices that ought to be made on moral or ethical grounds of one sort or another.

It is not only people with the moral stature of a Mahatma Gandhi or a Nelson Mandela who are concerned about the state of modern society. Even business leaders feel compelled to confess that there is something wrong with the present state of affairs. George Soros is one example among several who has made this observation about society in general: "Unsure of what they stand for, people increasingly rely on money as the criterion of value.

What is more expensive is considered better. The value of a work of art can be judged by the price it fetches. People deserve respect and admiration because they are rich. What used to be a medium of exchange has usurped the place of fundamental values, reversing the relationship postulated by economic theory. What used to be professions have turned into businesses. The cult of success has replaced a belief in principles. Society has lost its anchor" (Atlantic Monthly, February 1997). Business itself is beginning to recognise that the health of the planet and the quality of life of its people, the infrastructure on which it relies to do business from energy to transportation to water supply has become so complex, and so intertwined, that its vulnerability has increased exponentially and we are all at risk.

And so the ethics of living and making choices at this time in the history of our world are multiple indeed. They do affect every facet of our lives. The Club of Rome Report talks about "the ethics of nature, imposed by global environmental issues; the ethics of life exemplified by genetic engineering; the ethics of development, resulting from the increasingly unbearable gap between the rich and the poor; the ethics of money, because it is divorced from the economic realities and dominated the ambitions of too many individuals; the ethics of images, which should rule over media and modulate the influence of television in excessive dramatisation of the image; and perhaps the most important of them all, the ethics of solidarity, dictated by the fact of the dimension of the problems posed to mankind today requires co-operation between human beings as a condition of their survival" (Club of Rome Report, pp. 213-4).

Much of our world's suffering also seeps or explodes from the dangerous fault line that is the cleft between public virtue and private vice or public vice and private virtue. In other words, from a lack of integrity or wholeness. Integrity requires three steps: The first is discerning what is right and wrong. The second is acting on what you have discerned (even at personal cost), and the third is saying openly that you are acting on your understanding of right from wrong. Wherever we are in the world we must be aware that we are living on an imperiled planet: one desperately in need of ethical and ecological healing.

A University education should give the ability to discern that some beliefs, some ideas and some acts are ethically sounder than others and act on that discerning. The University is by origin and nature a universal institution and should be concerned with global issues and problems. The frontiers of the Universities are simply the frontiers of knowledge, the boundaries coterminous with the boundaries of the civilised world.

Conclusion

I know no better way to conclude my reflections on the Role of the Universities in Fostering a Harmonious Global society than by quoting Rabindranath Tagore's oft quoted poem:

> "*Where the mind is without fear and the head is held high*
> *Where knowledge is free*
> *Where the world has not been broken up into fragments*
> *By narrow domestic walls*
> *Where words come out from the depth of truth*
> *Where tireless striving stretches its arms towards perfection*
> *Where the clear stream of reason has not lost its way*
> *Into the dreary desert sand of dead habit*
> *Where the mind is led forward by thee*
> *Into ever-widening thought and action*
> *Into that heaven of freedom, my Father, let my country awake.*
>   *(Gitanjali, 35)*

Multi-cultures in Education and Collaborative

Inter-faith Educational Programmes

Bhu Dev Sharma

Humanity, we can all agree, is undergoing a major paradigm shift. Also this change is so fast that we have a tendency to see it in terms that have been left behind by events. There are several aspects of it. Out of the several matters drawing attention of frontline social/political thinkers, there is concern about nature of individual and his or her relation to the social order wherein concern with distributive justice (Rawl: Theory of Justice, 1972) is being replaced by 'identity question'. Another is the concept of human dignity in democratic order, appropriate to social diversity created by multiculturalism and feminism. A third one is the increasing importance of global at the expense of national.

In the context of present 'consultation' we need to join a debate on social shifts and inter-faith mechanics or multicultural scenario arising from these shifts.

In the first instance, my submission is that globalisation is not a global phenomenon. In fact, some countries have taken a reverse course by declaring themselves theocratic states and by imposing strict cultural laws, punishing the non-conformists. Bangladesh proclaimed itself as an Islamic country not too long back and Germany has, to an extent, not too long back framed laws favoring Christians. Thus, in the true sense, social globalisation is to be found only in·some countries.

Further, it may be recalled that, in the past also, there have been several phases of cultural shifts in different parts of the world. These, like spread of Buddhism in many parts of the world were peaceful while many others were violent and bloody. The phase of colonialism, perhaps also brought different cultures together.

Multiculturalism presupposes existence of many social/cultural groups in a place or country in which they exist together. If these social groups do not mix together, respect each other, understand each other, then this does not constitute multiculturalism. In this context, we need to understand what a social group means. Without attempting a formal definition, it may be said that a social group involves first of all an affinity with other persons by which they identify with one another, and by which other people identify them. Indeed, there are many cultural groups in the world. Their nature and histories are different. Existence of a multicultural society does not mean their peaceful coexistence. In fact, in most cases one finds conflicts and antagonism between cultural groups existing side by side. Also, world is witnessing a new phase of culture assertiveness, often violent. The state of clash of cultures is being analysed as the next power game in the world. Assertive groups, without knowing the strength of others, feel that they have the material and behave as though they have the right to speak and of being heard of.

In the past whenever cultures came in close touch, the result has been one of the following—assimilation, co-existence, confluence, extermination, deculturisation, or dehumanisation. History records every one of these along with the changes and sufferings every one of these brought about. Apartheid and slavery have been the glaring case of dehumanisation, while colonisation that of deculturisation. So called 'new worlds' present examples of racial extermination or racial cleansing.

It may seem that extermination, deculturisation and dehumanisation no longer exist, but my submission is that it is not so. These are not fully annihilated. Chechnia's civil war is recent example of attempt at extermination. There are tribal conflicts and racial cleansing going on in several countries of Africa, Asia and Europe. Examples near the home are that of Pakistan wherein half a century Hindu minority of 20 percent at the time of partition has been exterminated to less than 2 percent, and in Bangladesh, where the process continues, from 30 percent to less than 15 percent. My fear is that these may raise their ugly heads somewhere and sometimes unless the forces against them have struck decisive victory over them.

For multicultures to have an assured existence, several things need to be done. There are perhaps following type of multi-cultural societies:

- Traditional Multicultural societies, like India, Srilanka
- Emerging Multi-cultural societies, like USA, Canada, Australia, Brazil.

Traditional multicultural societies, like India have peculiar history of mutual goodwill and co-existence of different cultural groups. It is attributed to the spirit of tolerance and accommodation in the majority Hindu community. The educational system of India avoids teaching about different cultures. People understand them traditionally. Tolerant major culture accepts and respects other cultures. While there is perfect mutual goodwill amongst other religious groups, conflicts between Hindu and Islamic cultures exist and erupt occasionally. A major reason for current conflicts is historical partition of India in 1947 and creation of Pakistan on the basis of religion.

The emerging multi-cultural societies have preferred the process of assimilation some times referred as melting-pot model. However, this has lead to deculturisation more than anything else. In the postmodern phase, it seems that in USA there is a shift towards mutual co-existence of cultures. However, it is a society in full gear and media being powerful, stereotypes exist and major cultural group here has very poor or distorted view of other cultures. A common American does not know about Hinduism and one may find many who do not distinguish between Hinduism and Islam.

Some conflicts are perhaps natural and inbuilt. For example, there are cultures having very different attitude towards modernity, liberal democracy, status of women, and secularism. This is matched by the trend in the countries themselves while most of South Asia is democratizing, Pakistan is mimicking a Persian Gulf dictatorship.

It seems that a process called 'globalisation' is emerging. Societies that have values and traditions poles apart are coming in close contact. One witnesses a new kind of adventurism. The golden principle is: "you need to build coalitions." However, those coalitions are not without costs, and their models have not emerged. It may be noted that while scientific outlook is bringing people together, political and economic factors are the major players. Collapse of communism has seen vindication of capitalism. Role of and rush for money has changed attitudes and aspirations of people worldwide. Every area of activity has become career oriented. There are new trends. A Chinese youth is hankering for proficiency in English, and an Indian for Computer savvyness.

It is considered that the conflicts are caused by lack of proper understanding of others. This is, no doubt a viable hypothesis. To the extent this is the cause, a proper education can help in building goodwill among different cultural groups. The questions that arise are those that begin with what, where and who of such an education.

Teaching Hinduism presents special difficulties. The subject matter is very wide and varied. The instructors teaching Hinduism in USA are, practically all non-Hindus and, their anti-Hinduism is evident. Injudicious materials of study, biased presentation of Hinduism are common features. Hinduism courses are often taught in a way so as to create a revulsion against Hinduism in the minds of the students. Few examples may be useful:

- In Fall 2001, an Indian student (born in USA) took an introductory class in Hinduism at the University of Wisconsin (at Madison) and was shocked to hear the instructor describe the gory details of Asvamedha in the very first class. The students were told in the very first class that the chief queen grasped the penis of the dead horse and thrust it into her vulva and so on. The student was stunned and wrote that this does not motivate him to take any class on Hinduism in future now, even though he was well aware that there were several beautiful things in Hinduism and that the Asvamedha rite was performed very rarely, with these gory details probably often left out. In the last 2000 years, there are perhaps no more than 6-7 recorded instances of the rite being performed, and the last was performed at Jaipur in 1716. According to the *Dharmashastras*, it is in the category '*Kalivarjya*' and therefore its performance in modern times is prohibited by several Hindu texts themselves [See FUCHS, Stephen. 1996. The *Vedic* Horse Sacrifice in its Culture-Historical Relations. Inter-India Publications: New Delhi].

- A course book on *Ramayana* developed by Professor Susan Wadley at the Rochester University depicted Lord *Rama* as an Aryan imperialist, dalit oppressor, misogynist and a racist. The workbook sounded more like a rant of a Christian missionary. See what she wrote for US school students about Lord Ram and *Ramayan*:

"The rulers who control all knowledge, claim the *Ramayana* to be India's history and called us many names— demons, low castes, untouchables. But we were the aborigines of this land. Listen to our story. Today we are called the dalits, the oppressed. Once the *Aryans* on their horses invaded this land. Then we who are the natives became the displaced. Oh *Rama*, Oh *Rama*, You became the God and we the demons. You portrayed our *Hanuman* as a monkey, Oh *Rama*, you representative of the *Aryans*. You enslaved us to form a monkey army, those you could not subjugate, you called a *rakshasa*, a demon. But we are the forest *rakshak*, the protectors. You invented the hierarchy of caste through your laws of *Manu*, the first man. Oh *Rama*, you representative of the *Aryans*. And you trampled on the rights of women. You made your wife *Sita* undergo the ordeal of fire to prove her chastity. Such were your male laws, Oh *Rama*. Oh *Rama*, you representative of the *Aryans*.

When *Shambuka*, the Untouchable tried to gain knowledge, you beheaded him, Oh *Rama*. Thus did you crush those who tried to rise above their caste. Oh *Rama*, you representative of the *Aryans*. Days passed, years and centuries, but our lives remained the same. We skinned your cattle, So that you can wear shoes. We cleaned your gutters, so that you can stay clean. Oh *Rama*, you representative of the *Aryans*. Did you ever even ask, Oh *Rama*, what our caste is? Did you ever even ask what our religion is? Oh *Rama*, you representative of the *Aryans*. Independence dawned. It began with the rule of the constitution. The author of the constitution, Dr. Ambedkar framed the constitution around secular ideals. The castle of caste privileges began to crumble. No longer could the elite skim the milk of religious exploitation. Oh *Rama*, you representative of the *Aryans*. But poverty grew and to divert the poor from their real need, a new enemy was found. Muslims were targeted and "taught a lesson". To destroy Lanka, Oh *Rama*, you formed us into a monkey army. And today you want us, the working majority, to form a new monkey army and attack Muslims. Oh *Rama*, you representative of the *Aryans*."

In 2001, at the University of Michigan (Ann Arbor), the instructor of an introductory class on Hinduism gave a list* of suggested URL's for study to his students. In this list, there is only one site on Hindu women, and that site is so rabidly anti-Hinduism that its inclusion is shocking. There is an inclusion of anti-Hinduism sites by so called Dalits. (In reality, Christian demonstrably maintain many of these sites. An Islamic fundamentalist in the US, as is clear from the sponsorship, a sister site even lauds Osama bin Laden! The Government of India has filed a case of sedition against one of these websites.

The texts on Hinduism developed by Western Indologists dwell lavishly upon a certain set of topics that are a big turn off to students interested in Hinduism. These topics are caste discrimination, *Tantric Sex*, *Sati*, dowry deaths, polytheism, Hindu fascism, Cult of *Kali*, naked *Naga Sadhus*, which tend to give a biased view of Hinduism as a tribal, primitive, misogynist cult that has imprisoned millions of human beings. In net result, these books achieve exactly what the Baptist pamphlet on Hinduism does.

---

*   This list is available at http://listserv.liv.ac.uk

There is documented reason to believe that many Professors teaching and researching on Hinduism treat their 'objects of study' with contempt and condescension. According to Wendy Doniger, (She is a very powerful person in the field of *Vedic*, Hinduism studies, occupies a chair at the University of Chicago. (She was past President of the 9,000 strong American Academy of Religion, AAR). The '*Gita* is a Dishonest Book.' Her Ph.D. student, Dr. Jeffrey Kripal, who got appointment at Harvard University, recently, makes a child molester out of Swami Ramakrishna Paramhansa. Dr. Sarah Caldwell finds widespread latent homosexuality amongst Keralite Hindus.

Inter-faith education has major challenges, in India and abroad. It requires what seems rather impossible: no faith claiming exclusivity, superiority and there being moratorium on forced or motivated proselytisation. Perhaps the other way to partially achieve the aim is to have strong inter-faith dialogue in which one understands faith in others in the spirit in which its followers understand. It seems that in making a start it is the second scenario that has to be tried very diligently. The researches need also to be channelised in the spirit of building bridges.

The challenges in India require careful reorientation of education. There is a galaxy of Indian educationists and public figures to dwell on that aspect. Learning other faiths and cultures has two main processes:

1. formal in schools, colleges, and universities, and

2. non-formal—through films, meetings, media, conferences, ashramas, visits of holy persons, discourses, think-tanks.

The non-formal part is assuming greater importance in this age of electronic communications. There are already many good websites on Hinduism. Steps have to be taken to get rid of frivolous websites. Media projection of India is not only poor but in bad state. For countries outside India, strong cultural exchanges also have significant role in this non-formal process. Website material has started having powerful influence on formal education and this is on the increase. The days of the whole education system through schools, colleges, universities and institutions is looking for major change in pattern under the influence of web-technology.

With some experience, of about 23 years abroad in Caribbean and USA, I like to share some thoughts on proper formal teaching of Indian Culture and Hinduism in Western societies. Currently, most of the persons undertaking higher studies and research on Hinduism are non-Hindus. So as illustrated above, this is leading to major distortions. This needs correction in whatever way possible.

In Trinidad and Tobago, it is rather well taken care of by people of Indian descent. In that country of about 1.3 million people of which about 45 percent people are of Indian descent, they have started over 50 schools of their own, and enthusiastically observe their tradition publicly and privately. A cultural attache in Indian High Commission in Trinidad, and two chairs, one in Social Sciences and the other for teaching Hindi at the 'University of the West Indies' are capable of serving the cause well. The society is also having interactions with India through visits and conferences.

Amongst the other western countries, the four countries where Indian presence is felt are USA, UK, Canada and Netherlands. Here people of Indian origin, have a role to play perhaps as much, if not more, as the Government of India (GOI) agencies, like ICCR. The crux of the problem here is of finding right curriculum development, production of books and other instructional material for different levels—primary, middle, high schools and universities. School level teaching is the first to be attempted. This needs teacher's training in addition to preparation of material. This task needs scholars and resources to handle it for students of different cultural settings. This effort has been stepped up in USA after the September 11 (2001) incident, which has created a new urge in Americans to have a better understanding of other faiths, particularly Islam. Hindus are putting forth their case as well.

University level is not the easy part. Creating endowed chairs of Indian Studies have not served the purpose at all. Universities in those chairs appointed scholars of the kind whose examples are given above. In the name of academic freedom, university professors are teaching selective, outmoded, frivolous material.

Some societies, like 'World Association for *Vedic* Studies', 'Indic Traditions', 'Infinity Foundation', 'NFIA', etc. are actively involved in projecting correct image and in developing dialogue between scholars of the East and the West. It is also felt that, like Jews and different denominations of Christians, Hindus should found their own universities. Hindu University of America, Orlando, is one such step, which has been slow, unproductive and ineffective so far.

National Integration through Education

Ezekiel Isaac Malekar

India is perhaps the most pluralistic country in the world, and therefore India has the right pride of being a land of religions. The Gandhian ideal about religions can be described as that of "Republic of Religions" because India is mother of all religions. Living with diversity is one of the greatest challenge facing societies in which our children are growing up. We always believe in Vasudhaiva Kutumbakam. The World is like one family (Universal Religion). Cows are of many different colours but the milk of all is of one colour—white. Similarly seven coloured rays (rainbow) merge in white light.

Among the various countries, India is regarded as great because this is the land of duty in contradistinction to others which are lands of enjoyment, i.e. based on rights.

Mahatma Gandhiji eulogised this idealism in the following words:

"India is to me the dearest country in the world, not because it is my country but because, I have discovered the greatest goodness in it. Everything in India attracts me. It has everything that a human being with the highest possible aspirations can want. India is essentially Karmabhumi (Land of Duty) in contradiction to Bhogabhumi (Land of enjoyment)" (My Picture of Free India, p.1).

The words echoed in the historical memory of the nation, the first Prime Minister Pandit Jawahar Lal Nehru speaking in the Constituent Assembly at midnight on 14th-15th August, 1947 said :

"Long years ago we made a tryst with destiny, and now the time comes when we shall redeem our pledge, not wholly or in full measure but very substantially."

"Have we, 54 years after Independence, done enough to redeem that pledge? Has our pledge to the people of India, that their rights to life, liberty, equality and the dignity of the individual as guaranteed by our constitution, been redeemed? Even after 54 years of independency 500 million Indians are illiterate and about 100 million children in the age group of 6-14 years are at present not attending school. According to the World Bank, 54 per cent of the world's illiterate population in the age group of 15-19 is in India.

What is Education?

What is Education? Swami Vivekananda in "India and Her problems" explains: "Is it book learning? No. Is it diverse knowledge? Not even that. The training by which the current expression of will are brought under control and become fruitful, is called education. True education may be described as a development of faculty, not an accumulation of words, or, as training of individuals to will rightly and efficiently."

The ideal of all education, all training should be man-making. Education is not the amount of information that is put into your brain and runs riot there, undigested, all your life. We must have life-building, man-making, character-making assimilation of ideas. Education is a process of social engineering. In this process social, economic and other factors influence the education system and education leaves its marks on those factors. Indian civilisation recognises education as one of the pious obligations of the human society.

Dr. S. Radhakrishnan in his work, "The Principal Upanishads", in the course of his treatise on Taittiriyopanishad quotes what Patanjali said about education. "There are four steps or stages through which knowledge becomes fruitful. The first is when we acquire it from the teacher. The second when we study it. The third when we teach it to others and the fourth when we apply it."

It is sufficient to quote the following verse composed by the great Sanskrit Poet Bhartruhari of the First Century B.C.

"Education is the special manifestation of man. Education is the treasure which can be preserved without the fear of loss. Education secures material pleasure, happiness and fame. Education is the teacher of the teacher. Education is the friend when one goes abroad. Education is God incarnate. Education secures honour at the hands of the State, not money. A man without education is equal to an animal."

Aspects of Education

Patanjali highlighted four aspects of education to be accomplished with the directives to every individual being:

1. Acknowledge knowledge/education from your parents and teachers,
2. Make your own study and improve the knowledge,
3. Impart value added knowledge to other individuals, that is, to your own children as parent and to others as teacher or in any other capacity, and
4. Use that knowledge for family benefit, as also for the benefit of the society through your profession, vocation or employment.

Importance of Education

There is another verse in Hitopadesha which eulogises education:

"Education imparts intellectual culture; Intellectual culture secures capacity and stability; Capacity and stability enable to secure wealth; Wealth as secured enables to conform to *Dharma* which in turn secures happiness. Education provides hope for the modelling and shaping of the conscience and values of the future generations."

The everlasting value of education is also highlighted in Subhashita, thus:

"Providing education is of greater value than providing food, for satisfaction secured from food is short-lived whereas the satisfaction secured from education remains throughout life. The aim of education should be the all round development of personality intellectual, mental, moral, physical and to make an individual an asset to the society. It is only when a nation or society is able to achieve success in creating substantial number of such individuals, it secures happiness."

Spiritual Knowledge

Swami Vivekananda said that the spiritual force emanating from India will permeate the whole world, turning the current of men's activities and inspirations.

To recognise Ultimate Reality requires knowledge, not conceptual knowledge, but knowledge to be practised in life, to be understood by the heart, and to be realised in spirit. It is divine knowledge, as revealed in scripture or imparted through the teachings of people who have realised truth. Education and dilligent study elevates and enables the human reason. The most important knowledge is spiritual knowledge, which not only enlightens the intellect but also elevates the spirit and fosters good will.

There is no great wealth than wisdom, no greater poverty than ignorance; no great heritage than culture. Knowledge makes a man honest, virtuous and endearing to society. Knowledge is the holiest of holies; the god of gods, and commands respect of crowned heads.

All religions distinguish between intellectual study and the apprehension of spiritual knowledge that is conducive to salvation. For all its utility in the world, it does not profit the spiritual seeker, and may even impede the realisation of Truth.

Human Rights Education

The importance of Human Rights Education has now been widely acknowledged. Human Rights Education is essential for the full development of human personality for the promotion and achievement of stable and harmonious relations among communities and for fostering mutual understanding, tolerance and peace. It helps in inculcating those human values which shape a civilised society and strengthen a democratic polity. For these reasons, there is strong need for human rights education.

Human Rights education is not an end in itself. It is a means to secure the full development of human personality, social development of human personality, social solidarity, environmental safety, sensitivity towards both domestic and world public orders and international peace and security. In that sense, human rights education can serve its purpose better by encompassing the education and awareness about the importance of the rights of future generations, as well as the rights of animals, plants and trees. This will strengthen not only the spirit of humanism but also the natural foundations of human rights.

Value Based Education

Mahatma Gandhi had foretold what would be the fate of our nation if value based education is not provided after securing freedom:

"We should remember that immediately on the attainment of freedom our people are not going to secure happiness. As we become independent all the defects in the system of elections, injustice, the tyranny of the richer classes as also the burden of running administration are bound to come upon us. People would begin to feel that during those days, there was more justice, there was better administration, there was peace, there was honesty to a very great extent among the administrators compared to the days after independence. The only benefit of independence, however, would be that we would get rid of slavery and the blot of insult resulting therefrom.

But there is hope, if education spreads throughout the country. From that, people would develop from their childhood qualities of pure conduct, God fearing and love. *Swaraj* would give us happiness only when we attain success in that task. Otherwise, India would become the abode of grave injustice and tyranny of the Rulers."

Environmental Values

We are one earth community, one human family, and we share one destiny. We cherish and respect the rich diversity of life and celebrate the beauty of the earth. The earth community is our great gift and sacred trust. The vision has been distorted. Now life of the earth community is threatened with destruction. In the name of human progress and development, there is growing devastation of nature. People can be both the protectors and destroyers of the environment and their perceptions are extremely important particularly in a democratic society like that of India.

Inter-faith Organisations

"The 20th century has seen much bloodshed where religious differences have been a fundamental factor. But today number of Inter-faith movements exist with the explicit purpose of fostering a better understanding of religious differences and similarities. Through nurturing spirit of friendship and reconciliation, true dialogue can help us to overcome religious divisiveness and create new conditions for greater fellowship and deeper communion. It can help us to recognise that faiths other than our own are genuine mansions of the spirit with many rooms to be discovered rather than solitary fortresses.

Role of Teachers

Education is seed and root; civilisation is flower and fruit; cultivator sows good and wholesome seed; his community will reap sweet and wholesome fruit; if bitter and poisonous; then bitter and poisonous. Our cultivator, our culture-maker is the teacher. That he/she may cultivate well and wisely, he/she should be a "Man of God", *Brahmana, Maulavi, Pandit, Rabbi.* He/she should be a missionary of God; not a mercenary of *Satan.* Educationists in particular should bear in mind the fact that pupil is a unity of intellect, emotion and physical body, and that education only is good which informs the intellect with true and useful cultural as well as vocational knowledge, disciplines the emotions and the will into a strong, fine land, righteous character, and trains the body into a healthy, active, handsome shape and occupational skill.

The following famous sanskrit verse which the students were made to recite while commencing study eulogised the importance of teacher (*Guru*):

"My obeisance to *Guru* who is *Brahma* (the Creator), *Guru* (Teacher) who is *Vishnu* (The Protector), *Guru* is Lord (*Parmeshwara*), the sustainer himself."

The high respect accorded to the teachers shows the great importance given to education/knowledge.

National Integration through Inter-faith Education

National integration is the crying need of the hour. Every effort should be made to create emotional integration and a sense of unity. Publicity through every known medium is essential. This process of educating the public opinion should begin early in life. Through schools and colleges, the young men should be taught that the whole of India is one. Indian culture is basically one and the differences are only superficial. The very mentality of the young should be changed. Text books should be suitably revised. Oneness of the people, rather than the differences, should be emphasised. Similarly the radio, the T.V., the cinema and the press should also be used effectively to educate public opinion and develop national consciousness.

In India very little creative and evaluative attention has been paid to the media due to which its fullest potential in promotion of national integration has not been realised. All religious minorities receive respect and regard when their festivals and their religious events are around. But what the media is insensitive about is that these efforts do not contribute any way to inter-religious understanding or national unity.

Thus the media must plan for alternative strategies for national integration. The bhajan-quawali approach will not do. It has only made the minorities more cynical and has alienated them from the media. Thus one urgent step the media must take is not to simply confine the visibility of the minorities to *namaz* and prayers in mosques, churches or gurudwaras but give them greater exposure through various secular prgrammes.

Like education, mass communication too has met with very limited success in changing people's attitudes or leading them to action. The media can salvage the minorities only if there is available a rational, scientific and comprehensive cultural policy linked with the programme of social transformation of our society.

Inter-faith Education for a Global Society

Neelam Mehta

Till the event on September 11 (2001), little did anyone foresee the uncanny relevance this topic would assume soon after. The reign of terror unleashed by a handful of fundamentalists, with bizarre interpretations of a great religion has brought into sharp focus the urgent need for integrating the discipline of inter-faith understanding in the education system across the globe. The insanity arising out of misplaced beliefs about religious differences, has perpetuated the blackest era in the history of human civilisation.

Obviously, there has been a very grave oversight somewhere along the way, because of which the education system has not been able to hold the global society together on a premise of mutual respect.

Diagnosis religion, by its very definition, is a system of benign beliefs and practices. The underlying tenets of each and every religion are the same as any thinking, logical person will agree. If I say, "my religion preaches truth and kindness", is there anyone out there who is going to stand up and say, "but mine doesn't, or if I say, "my religion says love one another", is anyone about to say, "not mine". That being so, what in the name of God is going on?

The point of departure between one religion and the next, falls in the realm of rituals rather than value systems. These differences are healthy and indeed make for the spice of variety. The rich tapestry of civilisation is the interweaving of various cultures; their culinary, linguistic and ritualistic practices are interesting motifs that combine to make this tapestry more intricate, more colourful and more beautiful. The demented mind uses this relatively superficial aspect, rather than the real stuff religions are made of, twists and distortions to create a divide between peoples of different beliefs.

Accepting collective responsibility for the state of affairs is the first step towards any kind of correction. Each one of us, no matter which side of the divide, is guilty of omission if not commission. Had those of us who hold the view that religions are meant to bring out the best, not the worst in us, spread the spirit of inter-faith, respect them as much as the separatists have worked on their evil agenda, the balance may not have tipped so.

A two-pronged approach to mending the present situation can be adopted. On the one hand, the attitude of mutual respect needs to be forced in our day-to-day interaction. This attitude needs to be asserted at every available opportunity—be it in response to innocent questions of a child on innocuous discussion among friends or colleagues. The belief in equality of all faiths must be reiterated in strong terms. Whenever separatist tendencies raise their ugly head during a social conversation, at work or anywhere around us, we often overlook, either because we could not care less or in order not to rub the speaker the wrong way.

Taking a stand, without the slightest hint of aggression, is a precursor to creating an environment of healthy coexistence. The mindlessness of terrorism needs to be countered not 'out there' but in the domain of human psyche, which is exactly where the perpetrators of violence in the name of religion, have worked slow and long to realise their wicked designs. Ours too is a slow and long path, but a viable one.

Addressing the task at an organised level is the other prong of the correction strategy. The education system is the most potent vehicle for inculcating mutual respect and harmony. As we speed towards a global-environment it becomes imperative that we learn to allow for, and even appreciate viewpoints different from our own. There could be as many viewpoints as there are people in the world and each one valid. But rather than becoming the basis for conflict, that should open up myriad possibilities of seeing things from different perspectives of the world like a kaleidoscope in a child's hand with constantly changing patterns, each one more beautiful than the other. Imparting a wholesome curiosity for beliefs other than our own is a task that the education system needs to take very, very seriously.

Ignorance of each other's makes the work of the bigot easier. Most differences are created on the basis of hearsay rather than any genuine understanding of the premises in question. Armed with proper knowledge-difference between belief systems, an enlightened future generation can nip the forces of separatism at the nascent stage. And, this knowledge is best imbibed through the education system.

In the global scenario, knowledge of spiritual and religious practices of different faiths is as important as the study of History or Geography. A thorough understanding of the tenets of different religions will not only bring out the universality of all faiths but also make for reducing the possibilities of misinterpretation.

Some Suggestions

Religious Exchange Programmes pretty much on the lines of the prevalent Cultural Exchange Programmes, can go a long way in creating an awareness and even empathy for different faiths. Such programmes, promoted through educational institutions, would allow people the opportunity to "live" a religion off rather than their own for a period of time. This would enable them to understand the practices and the finer nuances of different religions and result in an appreciation of the strong points of the other faith.

Cross-Religious Discourses where a religious head or a celebrity associated with a certain religion, reads out portions of scriptures of another religion could be a very potent method for ensuring interfaith involvement. These discourses could be designed either to bring out points of similarity between the faiths or, even to rationalise points of departure with a strong emphasis on presenting them as two mutually acceptable points of view. The secular image of such a personality, of course, would be the most important prerequisite for the endeavour.

These thoughts are more by way of a starting point for evolving a long-term strategy towards creating an affable environment the world over. The organised endeavour will take a while to crystallise and to actually get implemented and integrated into the system. But the attitudinal shift, touched upon earlier in this paper, is an action that can be initiated with effect from this very moment on. Let each one of us 'wear' this attitude.

Holistic Thinking for Global Society

Rajni Tandon

Applied Humanism

Thought, by itself, is a silent, subtle, construct that selects and suggests an order forming synthesis to cohere distinct analytical entities. By extension, chains of thought get grounded in the search for harmony which ranges from simple cumulations to complex and compounded sets of situation related parameters. Since we humans are intelligence directed communicating inter-actors the awareness of parts entering into sets of flowing whole-spheres of action both define and confine the sociology of languages.

There are numerous energy potentials that qualify and quantify the perceptions that constitute our applied selfhood. The nature and functioning of different spoken, written, felt, known and sought languages become the basic unit for building the ever changing reality forming partnerships that manage our value processed working out of life.

In an audio-visually choreographed formation of diverse languages the focus on the socializing harmony of thought-as-action compels language users to delve deep into the spiritual recesses of striving to help each other in being and becoming better communicators. This paper opens out some holistic visions and versions of harmony building webs for framing sets of action- images.

The Design

Human intelligence has to be understood as a preoccupation with creation. Persons are benefactors and beneficiaries making and sharing benefits and benevolence in benign ways. The pursuit of benevolence is an invisible soul force that propels men and women towards seeking and learning ways of playing out roles as partners, ever striving to manage life in better ways.

Human vision searches for and locates the part to be played by sets of participants as partners operating through a dynamic conceptualising of a role as a goal, a whole and an entry into and exit from an orderly flow of interactive life management. Outer conditions of concrete effort are governed by inner compulsions, known paths, position, time frames, significance, and chosen modalities.

The facts associated with conditional states and the major factors affecting them are set in frameworks of value, vision, and versions of action for working upon ways of progress in viable, equitable and sincere ways. A lot of guidance, guesswork, gratification, goodness and grandiosity affects the configuring of methods and modalities to express and implement the services that are imminent being in sets of partnerships.

The audio-visual media can cohere, bind, bond and blend this concurrent thinking into holistic maps for cohering, synthesizing and giving a synergetic value additive power to strengthen the efforts that make up our applied humanism.

Formations of value activate the life living transformations of ideas, feelings, making products for consumption, reveal ways of dealing with conditions and evolve ways of sharing creative expressions to interact and work out patterns of nurture. A value framework is an emotion charged driving force that generates concepts and notions about contributing to different actual or visualised situated encounters with nature, each other, and various living species. In accordance with commonly known and specially sought values, better conditions for growth are provided and consumable goods are made. Since memory is scenic, selective, segregative, stipulative and short-lived and emotion is intimate, intense, imperative, intuitive and impulsive, a fine blending and balancing of both has to be derived to harmoniously co-ordinate decisions for living a good life. A meditative reinforcement of essential needs, requirements, tools, techniques, forms, and boundaries associated with sets of interactivity to establish and enhance the essence of concern behind a partnership constitutes the good life.

Cosmic creation has to be comprehended before human sensibilities, strivings, sensitivities, securities, and the services they perform can become superior inter-intra life sustaining services.

The primary pattern meditated upon by the great sages who gave us *Vedanta* opens out the *Bindu* and the *Naads* through which the atomic cells move and grow, bond together, decay and recreate in endless plays of energy and consumption. *Panchabhutas* cohere or clash to emanate as *Tattwas* of formed order in submission to *Vadis* connected with the situated encounter. *Anuvadis* form the negative and unnecessary aspects of the dialectics and have to be rejected. Human doers of deeds follow the same principle as they decide upon what they should, and must do to serve which cause and purpose.

When we place the information we have, and can access, about conditional situation related subject and theme based inferences and references, we gauge the appropriate growth evocative contribution to be made as we ceaselessly strive to be and become better persons. Many interconnected loops of notional energy obey the logic of known form and social order for controlling the free abandon of the flitting psyche. We move forward by accepting certain kinds of advantages, making certain assumptions and by selecting the commonly accepted modalities to implement the loss/gain visions within which our interactions are placed. This is the Trividha always being tackled by human intelligence.

A triangle was used to depict the locking in of the options to hold the wise choice in place. Another traditional image is of two arrows making circles chasing each other but they functioned according to an invisible third centre of faith in the value of the deed. The darting snake with its flowing energy was imaged as a coiled collocation of Kundals (knots?). The dialogic has two other intrinsic dimensions, those of capability and the skills that create efforts to propel us forward towards actualising good growth.

Triangles gyrating upon axes of use or depicted as diverse sections of awareness became other pictorial designs for holistic thinking. In traditional paintings, sculptures and other art heritages the images familiar to the consciousness were depicted. Circular or square patterns, decorative plants, birds and animals, the sky, the rivers and the waves accompanied symbolic human figures.

Artists have always been more sensitive to the wonders and the mystique of the unknown spirit which structures the real world of deals, deeds, relationships, concerns and commitments in endlessly perceived, conceived, constructed, maintained and sustained patterns of expressions. Performed arts and literary works reinforced varieties of value systems to remind forgetful humans about imperative self-disciplines.

The wise sages who gave us our ancient wisdom built their messages about the soul in action by locating five dimensional philosophies for coping with and forming the ever-present impacts of the changing realities within which life functions. Panchadarshana was not only repeatedly revealed as the truth but also became the most efficient method for opening out perspectives to form paths for implementing apt roles within the recurring panchasthitis of birth, growth, decay, death and rebirth that cyclically affect all creation.

Numerous *panchakaranas* (reasons), panchagunas (qualities), panchasheels (disciplines), evolve the *panchakriyas* that are the outcome of the panchaindriyas (bodily manifestations), that open out our cosmically given *Karma-Dharma. Panchagyana* can become a suitable epistemological framework for the contemporary web paged knowledge that incorporates the fields, areas, features, dimensions and functions of life organisation in graphic ideolects. A web configuration can compose sets of facts and the conditioning factors that govern knowing. It can present the models that guide us, locate the responsibilities that lead us, suggest the harmonies that expand understanding and show us ways of obeying the ideals that control the languages through which "*karyakramas*" of service, struggle, sacrifice, skillfulness and support evolve personalities. *Panchadishas* become suitable slots to format pleasing, good, appropriate, effective, and beautiful ways of managing Panchadashas.

In order to simplify the binding and bonding of thought mapping we can use the term *Panchabhaga Dhyana*. With audio-visual web pages we can integrate the ways in which we compose situated encounters to deal with sets of circumstances, types of conditions, and reinventing our stored knowledge, in association with varieties of acquired skills to hold and release diverse kinds of situation managing action energies. At the focal centre of the web of discourse created for target receivers are the contents that reveal the fulfilling of survival needs for vital growth, that make the images that are right for the situation specific mental progress, that show relationships that deal with psychological tensions, that repeat the postulates that govern ethical-moral and civil social behaviour and open paradigms for better quality intervening during our interactive functioning.

A knowledge unit can traverse situation relevant theories in terms of working practices, workable constructs, loving concern, detailed analysis and collaborative effort. This five dimensional semiotic moves between areas of information, descriptions of events, indicators of excellence, past histories, and present realities as properties and procedures for evaluating strategies for all round growth. The power to examine, use, establish, enable, entrust, experiment and explore knowledge as experience for dynamic action needs many new specific task centered situation processing uni-trans and para disciplinary illustrative panchabhaga darshanas.

In order to understand what entails being and becoming a better partner one needs to observe many faculties in great depth. At some hidden innate level our fiery will reacts to the bright light of wisdom that reveals paths to attain prized goals. Many winds of energy transfer and transform awareness while the flowing waters of love sustain and maintain partnerships constituted upon the solid earth that is the ground upon and from which goods for survival are produced and distributed. Conflicts, difficulties, confusions, passions and positions seek super-ego dominance to make benevolent decisions in the split second thought options that are available during the dialogical possibilities within rapidly moving interactive dialectics.

A web page is an exercise in applied sociology because it can cut across different disciplines to capture unifying experiences that graphically represent social knowledge, social postulates, social practices, and ordain social confidence as per the social norms for performing social roles. The range between the direct, the subtle and the ideal impact is included in the configured webs multi-purpose many layered thought. The macro can be connected to the macro and the real can be linked with the infinite as *panchadhyana* designs pierce through the limitations of the written word.

The conjoint group parameters of identity consciousness and the framing in time of good and great interacting has enormous significance for designing holistic thinking. Instinctive searches for security, the sense of belonging, the need for approval, principle based critical discussing and loyal support to a cause lead the social consciousness to greater ranges, heights and depths of interactive endeavor.

Rules, regulations, regularities of rituals, rhythms of routine habits are contentment spreading ways for processing human rights while reaching out towards self realisation. The systems approach delves into time management for attaining the optimum utilisation of human resources. A harmonious balancing of leisure time, soul refreshing time with work for earning time is like the seasons that colour panchaikaranas.

Ethno-socio-linguistics is a vocabulary building field that can be developed to incorporate sets of audio-visual languages in terms of personal, family based, local, regional, national and global co-relationships. Multicultural impacts upon the individual within a unicultural milieu create cross-cultural confusions and these need to be addressed, debated and accepted to aid resolution and help in adapting to or establishing new practices. Transcultural conventions and extremist views of culture conditioning need very wisely mediated experiences which are non-personal and indirect but very dramatic. Abstract thinking and the reaffirmation of social values have always been used by religions to promote good living, give counsel and guide collectives of adherents towards higher ideals. The universal togetherness spreading dhyana for the local to global bonding being sought today requires advertising strategies to present a sustainable impact upon populaces. The spirituality of applied humanism is the new mantra for projecting messages of common welfare and well-being. Market driven power centres need dynamic panchadhyana units to reveal how stake holders can be benefactors and beneficiaries when they provide benefits and benevolence to primary, secondary, tertiary receivers. The analysis of fringe benefits and the rebounding of benefaction per se deserves many mind mapping dialogues. A folk simplicity can be captured in animated pictures and supported with couplets, sutras, story pictures, songs and simulated situational models to become an effective literature for audio-visual broadcasting.

Grades, gradations, governance, grace and gratitude are some dimensions of deep thinking for getting holistic gratification. A highly philosophic gamut of the important, the significant, the specific, the superior and the higher expectation governs the holistic search for living the good life. It is clear that a lot of patient, persistent, proactive stable and mature academically sound unit formations are required for making holistic maps that serve as distinct epistemologies for enhancing human resources.

Our Vedas and Upanishadas have opened life-long learning as prayerful mantras set into patterns for the repeated *Shravana* of the *Shruti* so that the *Smriti* can make the *Buddhi* a *Sadhana* of *Sadhanas*. This gives us the trust and the faith to overcome the pain and conflicts of the *Mayavi* world as well as get the Divine support to locate unified *Sahyogas* to attain *Shanti* and *Shuddhi*. Science has corroborated with facts and outlined theories to explain how particles of matter are transmutated by atoms of energy that release catalytic forces to transmute existence. The greater the awareness we acquire about energised radiation creating powerful impacts and possible evolution within a set of functioning structures, the easier it becomes to accept our unique personal gifts for establishing new ranges of growth.

The collocations, conations, and computations possible in audio-visual languages can be very effectively used to strengthen the impact of messages for mass receivers by exploring and updating traditional design features derived from sets of cultural heritages, including abstract versions of radiant symbolic imaging.

Time dimensions play a very important role in holistic thinking. The timing and timeliness of the good action can be visually highlighted as a movement that cut across impulses, plans, and exigent pressures to illustrate how the right option operationalises our selfhood when the goals of wholism direct discourse.

Frequencies, fractions, fictions and fragments in cohesion with feelings become an important set of panchadarshana holism. Briefs and beliefs need to be framed as bandspreads of bonding pertaining to varieties of functioning partnerships. Chances and challenges, contacts and contracts, concerns and sacrifices are some sub-themes that need to be highlighted.

Captions, comments, continuities, controversies and complexities can all be incorporated for teasing the intelligence into wider and deeper thinking about critical decision making for optimising sets of benefaction.

States of being, (birth, growth, decay, death and rejuvenation) are framed in many abstract hidden intuitions, intellectual trusts, intentional drives, interest based habits and instantaneous exigencies all of which seek the most careful consideration.

Evanescent images build foregrounds of endeavour set against backgrounds of conditions and indicate scenarios of probability resulting from versions of possibility. Rays and rows, boxes and bricks, stars and radials, branches and stems are some designs for designing compounds of distinct but concurrent perceiving. The use of colour codes and the humane art for editing images can reveal meanings to project the mechanics of work, and the machinations of workers. The polity of psycho dramatic languages, the policy of social polemics and the dialectics of dialogue are some principles of interactive skills to be known to web page communicators.

While doing post-production editing, segments of sequences can focus harmonies within knowledge contents. The search for material value, psychological conviction, ethical value and positive

social-personal growth can be set in distinctive colour codes.
Foreground actions can be set in backdrops of brown, red, green,
orange and blue to denote changing moods/needs/urgencies,
pleasantries/difficulties. Sounds and music, theme emphasising
symbols, vivid settings, culloquial speech styles give added value to
role-playing.

Audio-visual life projecting pedagogy is a constellation of
attraction that glints to illumine means and methods, modalities and
materials, man power and mastery, musings and might, mystery and
management to send messages of good or bad interaction. The soul
force of dedication and devotion behind decision-making is the
resource behind all the other resources that are deployed in ongoing circuits of action/reaction. The soul-spirit wisdom which is
refined and rejuvenated with prayer has been spread by great
religious leaders since time immemorial. The pattern needs to be
accessed again and again to remind weak human beings about the
powers they have, can acquire and exert.

A beginning for making academic-cum-activist displayed in the
web page mode can be made by all educational bodies if they
commit themselves towards fielding and funding applied humanism
to make sets of receiver based folder series which can set new
habits of holistic perceiving.

Contributors

Dr Karan Singh
3 Nyaya Marg, Chanakyapuri
New Delhi-110021

Prof Marmar Mukhopadhyaya
Joint Director, NIEPA
17B, Sri Aurobindo Marg
New Delhi 110016

Prof Susheela Bhan
Institute of Peace Research &
Action,
81, Gagan Vihar
Delhi-110092

Prof K.D. Gangrade
Vice-Chairman
Gandhi Smriti & Darshan Samiti
5 Tees January Marg
New Delhi-110011

Ms Zena Sorabjee
Chairperson
Baha'i House of Worship
Bahapur, Kalkaji
New Delhi-110019

Dr A.K. Merchant
Director, National Spiritual
Assembly of the Baha'is of India
Baha'is House, 6 Canning Lane
New Delhi-110001

Dr Sampooran Singh
House 586, Sector 10-D
Chandigarh-160011

Dr. Shashi Tiwari
(Reader, Maitreyi College)
54 Saakshara Apartments
A-3 Paschim Vihar
New Delhi 110063

Dr J.S. Rajput
Director, N.C.E.R.T.
Sri Aurobindo Marg
New Delhi-110017

Dr J Veeraraghavan
Director, Bharatiya Vidya
Bhavan
Kasturba Gandhi Marg
New Delhi 110001

Dr Steven Paul Rudolph
Educational Director
JIVA Institute, Sector 21B
Faridabad-121001

Shri Bodhpriya Jaibharti
Jt Secy, Temple of
Understanding
15 Institutional Area,
Lodhi Road,
New Delhi-110003

Shri G.P. Chopra
President, DAV Managing
Committee
B-217 Ashok Vihar, Phase-1
New Delhi-110052

Prof K. Mathews
Head, Department of African
Studies
University of Delhi
Delhi-110007

Prof Bhu Dev Sharma
President, World Association for
Vedic Studies
54 Saakshara Apartments
A-3 Paschim Vihar
New Delhi-110063

Mr Ezekiel Issac Malekar
Judah Hyam Synagogue
2 Humayun Road
New Delhi-110003

Shrimati Neelam Mehta
Bagatelle Communications
A 1/609 Ekta Gardens
9, I.P. Extension
Delhi-110092

Dr Rajni Tandon
17 Link Road
Jangpura Extension
New Delhi-110002

The Temple of Understanding

To promote understanding among the world's religions
To recognise the oneness of the human family
To achieve a spiritual United Nations

The Temple of Understanding was founded in 1960 to address the urgent need of our time for understanding among and about the religions of the world. It is the world's second oldest international inter-faith organisation, and began through the efforts of a distinguished group of "Founding Friends", including Eleanor Roosevelt, Pope John XXIII, U. Thant, Albert Schweitzer, Anwar el-Sadat, Jawarharlal Nehru, Sarvepalli Radhakrishnan, Sir Zafrulla Khan, Thomas Merton, and the Dalai Lama, all of whom assisted the founder, Judith Hollister, in manifesting her dream of a world inter-faith centre based in the United States.

The Temple of Understanding has been globally multireligious and independent since it was first established. From early in its history the Temple of Understanding pioneered inter-faith dialogue through the sponsorship of a series of "Spiritual Summit Conferences" in India, Switzerland and United States as well as a number of other conferences, workshops and inter-faith celebrations.

More recently the Temple of Understanding has launched the North American Inter-faith Network, which now includes over 125 inter-faith organisations in the United States and Canada. The Temple of Understan.ing has also collaborated with the Global Committee of Parliamentarians to develop the Global Forum of Spiritual and Parliamentary Leaders on Human Survival which held several significant inter-faith conferences around the world.

The Temple of Understanding maintains a strong commitment to the integrity of the traditions of the individual faiths, which it believes can only be strengthened by association, discussion and opportunities to worship together. World peace and, with growing emphasis, responsibility for the planet's ecology, are major concerns within a theological as well as an activist context of education and communications.

Dr. Karan Singh has been world Chairman of the Temple of Understanding for several years. The India Chapter, under his guidance, has opened Centres in a dozen important cities around the country including Ahmedabad, Bangalore, Chandigarh, Lucknow, Mumbai, Nagpur, Patna, Varanasi. The main aim of the Temple is to further harmony and understanding between the various religious traditions of the world so as to work towards a sane and harmonious global society.

For further information, or to become a member, you can write to:

The Temple of Understanding (India Chapter)
15 Institutional Area, Lodhi Road
New Delhi 110003 (Tel: 2461 6067, Fax: 2687 3171)